QUICK RETURN

COMPOST MAKING

THE *ESSENCE* OF THE SUSTAINABLE ORGANIC GARDEN

ANDREW E DAVENPORT

I dedicate this book to my wife, without whose love, help, patience, support and encouragement, this book would not have materialised when it did and may never have done so. While I 'locked myself away' our home was literally dropping to bits, half finished DIY jobs were abandoned, candles were burnt in the middle and at both ends and conversations revolved around compost! In the hope that our lives return to some kind of normality after completing this book, I promise not to talk about composting (too much) and mend the garden gate, finish off the kitchen, fit the fire surround, put the skirting boards on ...

'The Divinity within the flower is sufficient of itself'

QUICK RETURN

COMPOST MAKING

THE *ESSENCE* OF THE
SUSTAINABLE ORGANIC GARDEN

First published in the United Kingdom in 2008 by QR Composting Solutions

QR Composting Solutions, Newcastle upon Tyne, UK
www.qrcompostingsolutions.co.uk

Text © Andrew E Davenport 2008
Photographs © Andrew E Davenport and Graham Oliver

Design and layout: Ian Scott Design

Printed and bound in Great Britain by Sovereign Press

Printed on recycled paper containing 100% post consumer waste

British Library Cataloguing in Publication Data.
A catalogue record of this book is available from the British Library.

ISBN 978-0-9560087-0-1

Maye Emily Bruce (MBE),
born 3rd May 1879, died 25th November 1964.
As one of the founder members of the Soil Association and
innovator of the 'Quick Return' composting method, her
main aim was to, 'Give back Life to the soil, and thus
eventually abolishing disease in plant, animal and man.'
(Photograph courtesy of Mrs. P.)

CONTENTS

About the Author

Andrew Edward Davenport was born in Dukinfield near Manchester and is a keen organic gardener and compost maker living near Corbridge in Northumberland. In his other roles he is a husband, father, electrical engineer and DIY handyman. He has no horticultural training but he loves to be in touch with nature and exhibits a passion and enthusiasm for gardening and composting as a means towards providing a beautiful place to live and a sustainable, healthier way of life for his family.

FOREWORD

This book captures the fascinating and remarkable work of Maye Bruce, one of the pioneers of the organic movement. She was a true ambassador of the organic movement, recruiting members to the emerging Soil Association and spreading the knowledge of the importance of the health and fertility of the soil through her books and method of composting. The book carefully updates her user-friendly method of compost making for the 21st century whilst maintaining its integrity with a total respect and admiration for its remarkable inventor.

The work of Maye Bruce and her fellow composting pioneers is more timely than ever. Sales of vegetable seeds now outstrip those of flowers. Growing food at home is no longer just a hobby and growing sustainable food at home is an important way for citizens to become more resilient to the twin threats of climate change and resource depletion. The QR composting method can help the organic vegetable grower to manage their gardens and allotments sustainably, without the need for manure and other fertilisers.

The pioneers of the organic movement must have sometimes felt like they were swimming against the tide. That is what makes their history so engaging. Yet now, as organic principles offer real solutions to the challenges we face, their philosophy is just as urgent.

Patrick Holden, Director of the Soil Association

Acknowledgements

During the assemblance of facts, information and photographs for this book, the response and willingness to help from individuals, societies and associations alike have been overwhelming. Wherever the path of investigation has lead me, my queries and questions have been answered with selfless enthusiasm and cooperation. Information has transpired from the most unlikely leads and 'coincidences' appear to be more than coincidence! There are many people, without whom this book would not have been possible, who I wish to thank individually, and if I have missed any person, society or body from my list then please understand that this is not deliberate and I apologise sincerely.

Louisa, for her untiring kindness, help, support and enthusiasm throughout the project.

The Soil Association for allowing me access to their archive and for permission to publish information from the Soil Association Journal 'Mother Earth' and 'Common Sense Compost Making'.

Roger Mortlock of the Soil Association for his help and support.

Patrick Holden, director of The Soil Association, for the foreword.

Marisa Vaughan of the Soil Association for her friendly, thoughtful, non-stop support and help with the project.

Ben Raskin of the Soil Association for his excellent and constructive technical advice.

Mike Hedges and Indra Starnes from Chase Organics for their friendliness and help with all manner of questions and queries regarding the history of Chase and Q.R. composting and compilation of the chapter about Chase Organics.

Chase Organics for permission to publish information and photographs from their archive.

Alan Jessup for his help, encouragement and belief in the project from the very start.

Mrs. P. for her fascinating, interesting and amusing stories about Miss Bruce and without whom much of the previously unknown biographical information in this book would not have transpired.

Ron Silver for his unswaying, friendly cooperation, humour and excellent recollection of Chase history and events.

Carol Jackson from CADHAS (Campden and District Historical and Archaeological Society) for all the information, correspondence and cooperation and for their kind permission in allowing publishing of the information and photograph from their archives.

Mum and Dad for proof reading, encouragement, support and for being there.

John Paterson for proof reading, moral support and encouragement.

Duncan Wise for his professional and expert opinions, encouragement, proof reading, advice and help from the onset of the project.

Duncan Macqueen for the excellent advice, knowledge, proof reading and thoughtful help.

Ian Scott for his excellent and intuitive artwork and help beyond any expectations.

Graham and Donna Oliver for the superb photos.

Marcia Bodenham for her friendly help and information.

Julia Scott for her friendly interest and support in the project, reading and excellent article.

Lady Iliffe for her help in providing an excellent reference for Q.R. compost making.

The Bruce family members, most notably Mary Bruce, for forthcoming help with biographical information.

Paul R. Hughes for his help regarding the history of Maye Bruce and Norton Hall.

Pauline Allwright of the Imperial War Museum for her help and cooperation.

Eric Robson for his help and comments.

John for his last-minute help with the crop-spraying image.

Where references are made within this book to the 'soil food web', it is intended that this is not in any way connected or linked with any commercial body or activity.

Introduction

In a screening of the popular BBC TV gardening programme 'Gardener's World' during the autumn of 2007, the presenter Monty Don, himself a fine fellow of organic principles, explained to the viewers that the programme received more queries about composting than any other gardening subject. Initially, I thought that this sounded surprising since there are many topics within gardening that people could write in about, so why composting? Possibly, it was just general interest type queries about composting or people wanting a bit of advice. I was reassured to know that composting is such a popular activity and the British gardening public are keen to make compost. Then a worrying thought struck me that this was not just idle chit chat; there must be a vast number of people who were actually struggling to make compost in their 'miraculous plastic contraptions' that claimed all manner of fantastic results. I related to the time when I had been in an almost desperate position with my 'miraculous plastic contraption' otherwise known as a 'Dalek'; after a year of adding kitchen waste, grass clippings, screwing up cardboard, putting up with fruit flies and shredding newspapers, the contents appeared to be preserved rather than decomposed! The message came through to me loud and clear; this was a massive plea for help and I was gripped by an urgency to respond in whatever way I could.

It was good to see that the interest and the enthusiasm is already there to make compost, people know that making compost is good for the environment, good for their gardens and saves them money. But it was easy to see why a lot of people, after they had made all reasonable efforts, could be put off the idea of composting and kiss their compost bin goodbye. Composting is nothing new and has been practiced for many thousands of years, so why are we having problems? What we need is some real help. There is a job to be done and a gap to be filled in providing a reliable system of compost making for the gardener, allotment holder and even the farmer. This was one of the deciding factors that spurred me into action to write this book because I realised that there was help available by bringing to the composter's attention the remarkable composting system that was developed by Maye E. Bruce in the 1930's. It is intended that this book, as an introduction to the 'Quick Return' (Q.R.) compost-making system, will provide the information, the knowledge, the reasoning and the understanding that will bring results to the home compost bin, just as Miss Bruce's books did over sixty years ago.

I will start by telling you how I became acquainted with Q.R. compost making. Some years ago, my father-in-law had for some time been promising to give me an old book about gardening. One day, the book was produced as promised and I was pleasantly surprised to see that for an 'old' book the subject matter was organic gardening and farming. The book was published in 1949 and was titled 'Organic Husbandry, A Symposium' and was a treasure trove of articles and experiences contributed from authors, associations, publishers and institutes, most notably the Soil Association, all with one common interest: the belief in organic methods as a means of survival. Ironically, the book predicts the crisis that we now face in terms of our poor health and subsequent enormous National Health bill, problems associated with the use of herbicides, fungicides and artificial fertilisers, and false dependency upon unsustainable gardening and farming practices. The book explains many methods and facts about organic agriculture and horticulture, some which I had heard of, many that I hadn't. There was a section on composting that captivated me with an excellent article written by Albert Howard about his 'Indore Method' developed in the 1920's in India. The only problem was that it required plenty of fresh manure as a major ingredient in the heap which at that time wasn't readily available to me. Another article was written by a lady called Maye E. Bruce about the 'Quick Return' composting system and immediately caught my interest because it described a method of making compost quickly that didn't require animal manures and didn't require turning of the heap. This was excellent news! I read on and the article described the almost unbelievable results that were obtained. I was overcome with intrigue and curiosity but there was one snag; the method required the use of an activator made from herbs. The article gave places and addresses where to get it but the book was so old that I didn't even try to contact them. I decided to make the activator for myself which meant obtaining the herbs and making the activator from scratch. Some were easily obtainable such as dandelion and nettle but others such as yarrow and valerian were a bit more elusive in that I could only obtain seed which would mean waiting a long time before I could grow the herbs and make the activator. Eventually a break through came when a search on the internet revealed that the company who originally supplied the activator, Chase Organics, was still making and supplying it. I was overjoyed, quickly sending for a tub and subsequently I purchased a copy of Miss Bruce's book 'Common- Sense Compost Making' which filled me in on the finer details of the method. The compost has done everything Miss Bruce claimed and I have never looked back; those first experiences with Q.R. composting have changed my garden and my life. My wife says she has my father- in-law to blame for all this. In answer to this my father-in-law is also to blame for my wife!

Miss Bruce, as she was known to most people, was a 'compost guru' and was deservedly known as 'Queen of the Compost'. Her method gained great popularity through the 1940's; a popularity which continued through to the 1970s with her books selling untold thousands of copies and her method being adopted by many thousands of people all over the world. Miss Bruce was a founder member of the Soil Association and I believe she deserves more recognition for her achievements.

Time has passed by and knowledge of good sound organic gardening practices, such as Q.R. compost making, have been almost forgotten. In relatively modern gardening times, with the advent of chemicals in agricultural and horticultural practices, new methods are invented and initially appear to do the job but eventually the true price of such inventions raises its head, often with a vengeance. Many examples of this can be quoted such as the use of pesticides like DDT which, where they were applied, almost annihilated entire parts of wild life populations, with the effects taking decades to subside after it was banned. Even in the organic world we appear to fail to pick up on ideas that are sound in principle but are often ignored because they are 'old fashioned'. We live in a world where new ideas, change, innovation and high technology prevail but if something is not broken why should it be fixed? There is nothing wrong with development and innovation, it is in our genes to do so but there is good development and bad development, good innovation and bad innovation. Sometimes we must look to the past for our inspiration and ideas without the stigma of them being old fashioned, as indeed clothing fashions and trends do this without a shrug. Obviously there are good ideas from the past such as the bicycle and bad ideas such as the hydrogen filled airship. I believe that Q.R. composting sits with its feet firmly in the 'good ideas' camp and whilst it appears to be an old idea, in terms of the thousands of years of man cultivating the earth, it is still relatively new.

Never has there been a more crucial time for the gardener to make good compost and therefore never a more critical time to find a suitable composting method to satisfy the needs of the keen gardener or allotment grower who wishes to compost his garden waste. Growing organic food at home or on the allotment has become a high priority in many peoples lives; demand is outstripping supply of organic food in the supermarkets; buzzwords such as 'carbon neutral' and 'food miles' are common place.

In October 2007, *The Sunday Times* reported details of a £12 million, European Union funded survey, known as the Q.L.I.F. (Quality Low Input Food) project survey that was being carried out under the leadership of Professor Carlo Leifert on a 725 acre site at Nafferton Farm in Northumberland. The farm has been organised so that organic and conventional crops are grown side by side and to allow rigorous testing to be conducted to determine the physiological differences between the different farming methods. Whilst the survey has not yet been completed, early conclusions regarding the research claim that up to 40% more beneficial compounds (vitamins and antioxidants) were found in organic vegetable crops and up to 90% more in organic milk. Higher levels of minerals including iron and zinc were also found in organic produce. This certainly adds weight to the 'organic is better for you' debate, providing further encouragement to buy organic produce or better still grow it ourselves and save the food miles.

In the absence of good farmyard manure, which is often in short supply even to many farmers let alone the gardener, the most critical element to good home grown organic produce is the practice of applying good compost, without either good manure or good compost, successful organic gardening is difficult or almost impossible to achieve. Indeed, even if manure is available, you should compost your waste, make use of its benefits and add as much diversity to the soil as possible. The compost heap is the heart of the organic garden or allotment and is a fundamental requirement to the fertility of the soil and is the means to successful and healthy growth in flowers and crops and in turn to the animals or people that eat such crops.

Successful composting is often claimed to come easy by most of the books, magazine articles, leaflets and manufacturers' literature that are available to us. I have had more disasters with compost-making than I care to mention and have even been told by my wife to remove the offending item from the vicinity of the house! I have read many books about composting and tried their methods but it wasn't until I read Miss Bruce's book 'Common Sense Compost-making' and followed her method of 'Quick Return' compost making that I actually had my first real success. I'm sure that I am not alone in this experience. Miss Bruce's book is, in my opinion, one of the best books written about composting even if you choose not to use the Q.R. method that she prescribes. The methods and ideas detailed are timeless and the story of Q.R. composting and how she developed it from the herbs used in Rudolph Steiner's biodynamic methods, is a fascinating and compelling read. I have read her book a countless number of times and never tire of reading her gripping words. This book is not meant to be a sequel to Miss

Bruce's books and neither does it aim to 'outdo' Miss Bruce's work in anyway, indeed, I am a 'mere apprentice' in the art compared to Miss Bruce who had some where in the region of 40 years composting experience in her lifetime. My main priority is to relay the wealth of Miss Bruce's work and methods to the gardening generations of the modern world in the 'apparent' absence of anybody else having done so to date.

Despite common misconceptions, there is no point in making pretences that composting is easy and a simple matter of throwing things into a bin, leaving it for a while and then coming back in a few months to lovely compost. It doesn't work like that. There is no magic handle to turn or button to press. Mother Nature is in the driving seat; we have to respect the environmental and dietary needs of the organisms and creatures that make the compost. If we work against those principles then inevitably we will not succeed in what we set out to achieve and in extreme cases, create a foul-smelling, putrefying mess. This book can provide the composter with the intimate knowledge of how to work with nature and achieve the goal of dark, friable, sweet-smelling, nutrient-rich compost made within a few months.

My first success in making compost required a certain amount of investment in labour and materials to construct suitable bins, covers and drainage. Patience and tenacity were also required in following the instructions precisely. The important things that helped the system to work were shelter, retention of heat, aeration and good drainage. These are primary requirements for any good compost making system. Composting doesn't come easy at first but once you've successfully made compost it becomes second nature and failure rarely returns. The effort put into composting is paid back many, many, times over.

I believe the primary requirement for organic gardening and farming is the health and structure of the soil. Get the basics right and the rest should follow on. Regular addition of compost to the soil is one of the best methods of feeding and improving the condition of the soil and giving it the life and health it deserves. My garden has a heavy clay soil and used to be difficult to work, often becoming waterlogged in wet weather and the ground baked hard and cracked in the sun. However, with the regular addition of compost the soil has improved immensely; plants grow that wouldn't grow before, old shrubs have been given a new lease of life, the soil has a friable texture and plants take more readily to the soil, plants need less watering and weeds are easier to extract from the soil. Plants are more healthy, are more able to stand up to the elements and don't die through disease; chemical fertilisers, pesticides or other forms of pest control are not required. These are advantages that save time, money and most importantly valuable, environmental resources. Should we choose to grow our crops in such soils, we will also be rewarded with good health; a priceless commodity. Compost making is common sense as Miss Bruce's original works testify.

Miss Bruce introduced the Q.R. composting system as a means for gardeners and farmers to make their own high quality compost without the addition of manure and with an end result that equalled or surpassed other composting methods such as the 'Indore' method as mentioned previously. The distinct advantage with Miss Bruce's method being that the compost could be made quickly (hence the name 'Quick Return') and also with less effort due to there being no requirement to 'turn' the compost. Whilst turning compost can be a great advantage if you wish to keep fit, it can also become a chore and for busy or physically less able people it may not be feasible. There are many different types of composting and an ever increasing number of types of compost bin available in the marketplace with many claims about their performance. It is not an   objective of this book to discuss these methods and products since there are many books which successfully cover these topics.

When I set out to write this book my main aim was to enlighten gardeners and allotment holders, novice and expert alike, to the concept and advantages of using the Q.R. compost system as a sole method of making excellent compost. In effect, to pass on the legacy of Q.R. composting to today's gardeners that Miss Bruce has entrusted to us. Nothing has changed in terms of that objective. But as the book developed I started to think about a suitable title; it was then that I realised what was actually unfolding in front of me and it was something I could not ignore. The whole concept of what I had written about dawned on me; the Q.R. composting system was a perfect means of creating an eco system that can satisfy the criteria for the attainment of a sustainable organic garden. The book had a completely new singular meaning to it that brought everything together into a unity. I'm sure Miss Bruce was totally aware of what she had created, it almost went without saying but in today's world the impact of that meaning is much stronger and has possibly greater implications. I immediately realised the importance of these implications and how it could help the modern world.

Let's step back in time to 1940, when Miss Bruce wrote her original work, 'From Vegetable Waste to Fertile Soil'. The country was at war with Germany and the famous 'Dig for Victory' slogan was on the tips of everybody's tongues. It may be coincidental that she wrote the book and issued it just after war broke out but there could have been no better time to do it in the sense that every conceivable effort was needed if Britain and the allies were to suppress the advance of the German invasion of Europe.

Her composting method was promoted in 1938 by L.F. Easterbrook, the agricultural correspondent in the national newspaper, *The News Chronicle*, with hundreds of readers writing in wishing to know more about the method. Her work was also most devoutly supported by Lady Eve Balfour, the founder of the Soil Association. This support, coupled together with her determination, her friend-making personality, her influence and, most importantly, her successful method of composting, got her compost method the recognition and popularity it deserved. She made a considerable impact with her Q.R. compost system in those arduous war years, certainly making a valuable contribution to the 'Dig for Victory' campaign. In the opinion of some, it was the perseverance and determination in the winning of small battles such as this that ultimately decided the victors of that war.

Today, in 2008, there is a very different kind of war: the war on climate change; a war which many countries are still attempting to ignore, a war which could have world wide catastrophic consequences more severe than any previous war. Many people think that this isn't going to affect them and are burying their heads in the sands; there still appears to be a very adamant 'live for today' attitude and this is not just people in the street, governments in some countries are behaving in a similar manner. Whilst climate change has now been recognised by our government, it is failing to respond quickly enough to the recommendations of scientists' reports, such as the Stern Report, which recommends a 60% reduction of carbon emissions by 2050. If we are to achieve this then sustainable activities are required in all walks of life, not least in gardening and growing our own food.

During the writing of this book, I read a booklet published by the Soil Association titled 'One Planet Agriculture: The case for Action'. Alarmingly, the booklet informed that we are faced with another battle; the fast looming shortage of oil. The association for the Study of Peak Oil advises that "of the 65 largest oil producing countries in the world, 54 have passed their peak of production". 'Peak Oil' is defined as the day when the maximum amount of oil that can be supplied is reached. From that day forward that amount of oil can never be supplied again. There are reports that suggest that Peak Oil will be reached within the next couple of years. From the date that Peak Oil is reached, demand will be increasing further whilst oil supplies are reducing. Even if the reports are wrong, the day that this happens will inevitably arrive and it is highly probable that the impact will hit us before the major effects of climate change occur.

When Peak Oil hits us, demand will start to outstrip supply; eventually prices will rocket and curb our usage. We won't have any choice in what to do about it, we will have to take action. All products and human activities will have to be as sustainable as possible; we will have to cope with a radical reduction in fossil fuel inputs into all our activities. Whilst gardening may not appear to be that important in the overall scheme of things, the time will come when our gardens will need to produce food once again, as they did during the Second World War, when every bit of land that we own will become precious to produce crops. Sustainable organic gardening as a means of food production will become a must.

Apart from composting, there is no other single activity within the garden that can claim to accomplish so much towards achieving sustainable organic gardening. The Q.R. compost heap is the heart and hub of the garden where vitality and health is created. Diseases and weed seeds are eradicated in the intense heat (up to 70° C) of the Q.R. compost heap. All garden waste such as plant clippings and surplus commodities are turned into valuable compost. Old life gives rise to healthy new life. New seedlings and plants are given the start they need. Older crops, perennial flowers and fruit bushes are given a welcome boost. Health and vitality is given to the plants and they flourish in it, rewarding us with vivid coloured long lasting flowers and tasty, nutritious fruit and vegetables. But there is nothing new in all this; the Chinese have made compost for thousands of years and it is part of their tradition. Our predecessors swore by the 'rule of return' where all manures and vegetative waste were returned to the soil in order to feed it with humus; they were farmers who practised sustainability because they had to. Somewhere along the way we have chosen to ignore the knowledge and the skills to these simple practices and in the end we will have gained nothing other than learning the error of our ways. A new era has begun with the crisis that the world faces in terms of climate change and the more imminent problem of 'peak oil'. Whichever way we look at it, the sooner we localise, de-industrialise and make our activities sustainable, the more we can reduce the impact of these looming disasters and if we act soon enough we can stay ahead of trouble. In terms of composting and gardening, which is where this book is aimed, we should look towards composting as much of our waste as possible at home where it originated, feeding our soil with this to grow as much as possible of our own food. In short, the wartime slogan 'Dig for Victory' is as appropriate today in the war on climate change and peak oil as it was during the Second World War.

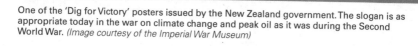

One of the 'Dig for Victory' posters issued by the New Zealand government. The slogan is as appropriate today in the war on climate change and peak oil as it was during the Second World War. *(Image courtesy of the Imperial War Museum)*

Hopefully, there will be something of interest in this book for anybody wishing to know something about Q.R. composting. Certainly, there will be gardeners who are already aware of the Q.R. system, possibly from its original beginnings with Miss Bruce, possibly recent converts or maybe those who have just heard about the method and want to find out more. The book highlights the significant factors and salient points of Miss Bruce's work and also provides supplementary information where necessary. This includes; additional history and background to Miss Bruce's life uncovered from recent research, scientific theories which enhance those put forward by Miss Bruce, the realisation of how the Q.R. composting system can achieve the *sustainable organic garden*, a 10 step quick reference method to aid the gardener in following the Q.R. composting method, information regarding the properties and uses of the special herbs used in the activator and a special chapter dedicated to the important relationship that has been forged over the years between Chase Organics and Q.R. compost making. In the interest of continuity, a method is also provided for the farmer since it was Miss Bruce's intention that the Q.R. method was introduced for farmers and gardeners alike.

CHAPTER 1

Portrait of Miss Bruce
circa 1951.
(Courtesy of Mrs. P.)

THE HISTORY OF MAYE E. BRUCE AND Q.R. COMPOST MAKING

The following chapter is a brief background to the life of Miss Bruce and her work. There is already a reasonable amount of knowledge about Miss Bruce's work from her second book 'Common Sense Compost Making'. The basic outline of the following story is believed to be the same and has been included for information and interest purposes within this book. Recent research has unearthed additional facts and information, biographical and work related, from sources including the archives of the Soil Association, Chase Organics archives and the Campden and District Historical and Archaeological Society archives (CADHAS). Mrs. P., who was the maid for Miss Bruce for 26 years, provided biographical information during interviews conducted in 2007. Kind permission has been granted for inclusion of material from all of the aforementioned contributors.

Throughout the book Maye E. Bruce is referred to as Miss Bruce which is not just a formality, I believe that many people knew her and called her by this name when she was alive.

Maye Emily Bruce was born in Dublin, Ireland, on 3rd May 1879, the eldest of seven children. From information supplied courtesy of CADHAS, it is known that her father, Sam Bruce, came from a Northern Irish distilling family and bought Norton Hall in Chipping Campden, Gloucestershire, sometime during the 1880's. From a family tree drawn up by one of her descendants, her father's family can be traced back to Robert the Bruce, first King of Scotland. Her mother, Julia Colthurst, came from the family who were once the owners of Blarney Castle near Cork in Ireland, and was also a descendant of Sir William Petty, the famous political economist, scientist and philosopher.

Little is known regarding her early years and youth but in her twenties, through her love of hunting, she became involved with shooting clubs. Her vigour and 'get up and go' led her to take an interest in the Church Lad's Brigade which introduced her to 'Lord Roberts' National Service League'; formed in the early 1900's to stir up the need for compulsory military service in answer to the unstable military situation in Europe. Miss Bruce was gifted with the power of public speaking; she had the ability to captivate an audience and she gave many speeches around the country, persuading people to join the league, contributing to the massive membership of 270,000 which was attained by 1914.

When her parents moved to London in 1912, Miss Bruce stayed in residence at Norton Hall and shortly following the outbreak of war, in October 1914, the Hall was set up as a Voluntary Aid Department (V.A.D.) Hospital, being one of the first establishments to do so. Miss Bruce was Commandant of the hospital which was staffed by voluntary nurses and stayed open until the spring of 1919. Deservedly she received an MBE for her work, as did all the other commandants who also received MBE's.

Her next venture brought her into the arms of the Girl Guide movement; she soon become a Commissioner and shortly afterwards she was made County Commissioner for Gloucestershire, a position which she held for 17 years. She retired from the position to allow a suitably younger woman to carry on with the work.

Miss Bruce was a lover of nature; she collected wild flowers and was interested in birds and butterflies. She also had many other interests; she was artistic, being a very good photographer, and painted and drew on occasions; she liked walking, mountaineering and travelling (she collected many books on this subject); her main interest and love was hunting which apparently she had an aptitude for.

Norton Hall was sold in 1921 and Miss Bruce purchased her own property, a neglected

Norton Hall, the Bruce family home, during the First World War when the Hall was set up as a Voluntary Aid Department (V.A.D) hospital. Miss Bruce is in the rear row at the centre. *(Courtesy of CADHAS)*

Miss Bruce (left of the dog) at the farm with the Girl Guides, during her days as the Gloucestershire County Commissioner. *(Courtesy of Mrs. P.)*

farm near Cirencester in the Cotswolds. The farm was overgrown but had good structure in its buildings and two magnificent trees overlooking the house and the farm. Initially, Miss Bruce used the manure from the farm to restore and bring life to the stony Cotswold soil, however, the manure eventually ran out and the farm became in desperate need of a replacement for the manure. As a means of producing compost, she had heard about the Anthroposophical Society through a friend and decided to join. The society based their work on the theories of Rudolf Steiner and Miss Bruce learnt the virtues of biodynamic compost making. Whilst she maintained a good relationship with the society, she had her own thoughts about the methods and decided to move on and follow her own ideas. Inspiration came in the shape of her theory that 'The Divinity Within the Flower is Sufficient of Itself'. Miss Bruce decided to experiment with the herbs that the society used which were not kept secret. What was secret was the method of preparation, however, even Rudolph Steiner had said 'For Heavens Sake experiment for yourselves'. She extracted the essences from the flowers and at a dilution ratio of 10,000 to 1, her activator produced a compost of excellent 'manurial' value, equalling that of compost made by the biodynamic method and Albert Howard's Indore method [1]. What made her compost even more special was the speed with which it was produced; Miss Bruce claimed the compost could be made in 4 weeks for a heap made in the spring, 8 weeks for a summer heap, 12 weeks for an autumn heap and hence she named her composting system 'The Quick Return Method'. Furthermore, because of the way in which the activator worked, the heap required no turning.

If Miss Bruce was to convince other people that her solutions (and method) were successful and would work for others, she would need some kind of impartial or independent testing to verify their worth. Julia Scott, of 'The Walled Garden' in Worcester (see Chapter 8 for further information about Julia and her garden), informed me that during the development of the Q.R. method, Miss Bruce had sent her solutions in small pots to an independent observer for testing. In the late 1970's Julia visited the herb garden of Stanbrook Abbey in Worcester (a closed order of Benedictine nuns), a garden where composting was 'par for the course' and prolific herbs were grown for kitchen and medicinal use. During this visit Julia stumbled upon the fact that one of the sisters, who ran the herb garden, had been appointed as Miss Bruce's independent observer. Miss Bruce had sent jars of material treated with different dilution ratios of the activator solutions with the intent of obtaining confirmation of their performance.

(1) The Indore method of composting was developed in the 1930's by Albert Howard during his time at Indore in India. The method uses layers of manure and vegetable matter turned at regular intervals.

The outcome of the testing is not known but one can assume Miss Bruce's findings were verified, judging from the subsequent publicising of the Q.R. method and the interest that ensued from gardeners and farmers alike.

In 1938, L F Easterbrook, the agricultural correspondent from the daily newspaper *The News-Chronicle* wrote an article about Q.R. composting which provoked a huge response. Hundreds of people wrote in asking about the compost and how it was made. This set the ball rolling, however at this stage Miss Bruce was still producing the activator in the form of solutions. The solution contained the flower essences of several herbs plus oak bark and honey. The honey had to be added to the herbs immediately prior to use otherwise the solution would ferment. This meant sending out the solution in two parts.

Miss Bruce's intention was to make the composting method available to as many people as possible. It was not her aim to gain from it financially, her primary motive was to 'Give back Life to the soil, and thus eventually abolishing disease in plant, animal and man'. It would also help gardeners and farmers make their own compost where manure was not available and vegetable waste was predominant.

In 1944 Miss Bruce had the idea of drying the herbs and making a powder which solved the problem of having two solutions and also made the packaging and shipping of the activator much easier.

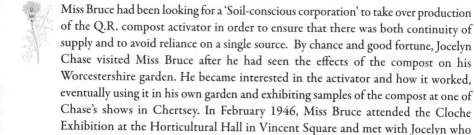

Miss Bruce had been looking for a 'Soil-conscious corporation' to take over production of the Q.R. compost activator in order to ensure that there was both continuity of supply and to avoid reliance on a single source. By chance and good fortune, Jocelyn Chase visited Miss Bruce after he had seen the effects of the compost on his Worcestershire garden. He became interested in the activator and how it worked, eventually using it in his own garden and exhibiting samples of the compost at one of Chase's shows in Chertsey. In February 1946, Miss Bruce attended the Cloche Exhibition at the Horticultural Hall in Vincent Square and met with Jocelyn who agreed to take on the manufacture and distribution of the activator and the company have played a vital role as manufacture and supplier of the powder for over 60 years (see Chapter 9).

Until 1946, Miss Bruce had been crushing the herbs using a pestle and mortar to make the Q.R. powder, however, according to Miss Bruce, one of the employees of Chase had the bright idea of mechanically grinding the powder which resulted in the following benefits:

- The quantity of powder required was slightly larger and possibly made it easier for people to measure out (a small teaspoonful)
- The powder was more dynamic and powerful in its use
- It was easier to handle

Miss Bruce claimed that using the new method of grinding the powder produced the best compost she had made. Her reasoning for this being that the finer particles would be more evenly and further spread around the surface area of the tubular holes that were made in the heap for the insertion of the activator.

The grinding and blending of the powder would be difficult for people who wanted to make their own in this manner, they would be better using the original method of crushing the herbs. Miss Bruce continued to sell her own crushed powder alongside Chase who supplied the ground version. Chase Organics still supply the powder to the original formula, selling thousands of packets per year to this day.

In 1940, when Miss Bruce wrote her book 'From Vegetable Waste To Fertile Soil' she had already been making Q.R. compost for some seven or eight years. England was at war with Germany and it is possible that she released the book in an attempt to get people composting as part of the war effort. The book was quite direct and brief, explaining the Q.R. composting method and theory extremely well, but lacks the personal charm and interest she provoked in her second book, 'Common-Sense Compost Making' published in 1946. This was an instant success and generated very wide acclaim. The book tells the story of Q.R. composting, partly set amidst the back drop of World War II when Miss Bruce was still able to carry out her composting experimentation and development despite the country being at war, probably because when the war started in 1939 she was already 60 years old and would obviously not be called upon for any war duties. But in her own way, Miss Bruce's contribution to the war effort was nonetheless valuable. Whilst she was not engaged directly with the enemy, so to speak, her efforts were at the 'front line' in terms of aiding the nation in the effort to grow their own food and maintain health by her promotion of the Q.R. method of compost making. All her staff were called up in 1940 and in their place she was left with a crippled old man in his 70's. 'Dig for Victory' was the message from the government and all efforts were concentrated on the kitchen garden (and composting!)

with the flower borders abandoned. The vegetable garden became a new area for development and experimentation with the composting where amazing results were achieved in the quality of the crops grown.

As far as the Organic Movement was concerned, the book was, probably coincidentally, released at a very critical time, being the same year that the Soil Association was founded by Lady Eve Balfour. I was informed by Mrs P. that these two ladies were extremely good friends and together they would attend farming shows, such as the Royal Show, taking with them samples of the compost in punnets and leaflets on how to make Q.R. compost. At the Royal Show in 1947, Miss Bruce had a small stand pitched next to a large I.C.I. (Imperial Chemical Industries) stand which had a large banner over it reading; 'FARMING TODAY'. Not to be outdone, Miss Bruce put up a banner over her stand reading; 'FARMING TOMORROW'. Even in those days there was an air of dispute between the organic and the orthodox (where artificial fertilisers and pesticides are used) approaches to farming and horticulture, with those in the organic camp being ridiculed as the 'Muck and Magic Brigade'. Whilst a lot of ground has been made since the early days of the Organic Movement, there is still a long way to go and hopefully Miss Bruce will be right one day in her concept that all the farming of tomorrow will be organic.

There is insufficient information to assess whether Miss Bruce had any bearing and influence in the formation of the Soil Association, however, it is known that she was a member of the early councils that were elected and was considered to be a founder member.

The first issue of 'Common-Sense Compost Making' contains details of the practical demonstrations which were commenced in 1940 at the Haughley Research Station (Lady Balfour donated her farm to the Haughley Research Trust and was the resident farm manager accepting the wages of a labourer). The experiment was set to test the disease resistance in stock animals when they were subjected to 3 different methods of nurture; organically manured, artificially manured and a mixture of the two. The testing was taken over by the Soil Association in 1947 and ran its course for over 20 years despite many difficulties encountered in maintaining funding.

Haughley was also to be the location of another test, this time it was the testing of Miss Bruce's compost in July 1946. Lady Eve Balfour wrote to Miss Bruce, asking if she would submit the Q.R. compost activator to scientific testing at the research station.

Miss Bruce at the Royal Show in 1947.
(From "Mother Earth" autumn 1947, courtesy of the Soil Association)

Miss Bruce accepted and the tests commenced with 3 heaps being built, based on the Indore method of composting, one of them being inoculated with the Q.R. activator. The details of the tests can be read in her book. The conclusion by Lady Eve Balfour of the compost produced was as follows: 'There is unanimous agreement on the considerably greater breakdown of organic matter and increase of humus formation in the treated heap. From the data already gathered it would appear evident, that at the very least, the inoculation of Indore Compost heaps with Q.R. Herbal infusion and soil will enable a saving to be made of at least one turn' The real proof came when the compost was used on the soil for the sugar beet crop of 1947. The report was written by Lady Eve Balfour and printed in the spring 1948 edition of *Mother Earth* (the journal of the Soil Association): 'The total average sown was six acres, but as one acre was very poor indeed, calculations have been made on a basis of five and a half acres. All yields were low in 1947, owing to the late spring followed by drought, but the half acre which received the Q.R. yielded at the rate of eleven tons per acre, twice the tonnage of the average of the whole field, and approximately two tons per acre more than the next best half-acre.'

Seven impressions of the first edition of the book were printed between 1946 and 1957. After her death in 1964, the copyright for the book was left by Miss Bruce to the Soil Association to which all royalties were paid. In 1967, Lady Eve Balfour produced a revised edition, which changed very little from the original texts. Some of the facts and prices in the book were brought up to date for that era and some changes were made to tenses. In her preface to the 1967 edition, Lady Balfour stated the case for vital food grown in compost as a means to improving the health of the nation and saving medical costs to the governments of the world. Public awareness was required before governments will take action and in Lady Eve Balfour's words, "Miss Bruce's prophetic voice; her enthusiasm, and selfless giving of her inspiring personality and the benefit of her personal experience were potent factors during her lifetime in helping to awaken this awareness".

The last edition of the book was published in 1973 and as far as I am aware its final reprint was in 1977.

In October 1951, there was a feature on Miss Bruce in *Mother Earth*, by which stage she was very well known and renowned for her work, influence and tremendous contribution to the work of the Soil Association. The article included a portrait of Miss Bruce taken especially for the journal. The article went on; "always a keen collector of wild flowers, she first worked out the idea of a simple herbal activator in 1935. She has been experimenting ever since, while the activator itself has proved a boon to many thousands of gardeners. It only remains to add that Miss Bruce's enthusiasm for organic gardening is of the highly infectious variety, that it has made her friends in every corner of Britain, and that her own beautiful Cotswold garden, with its fascinating compost 'Kitchen' is ample evidence that she practices what she preaches."

Miss Bruce was on the council of the Soil Association from spring 1947 to the end of 1961, only missing one council meeting in fifteen years which was apparently by accident. In a tribute to Miss Bruce's 80th Birthday which appeared in the April 1959 edition of *Mother Earth*, the author of the article (possibly Lady Eve Balfour) raised the question, 'Would there still have been a Soil Association without her faith and enthusiasm?' In times when the Soil Association encountered severe financial difficulties, Miss Bruce was always there, enthusing positive faith and confidence for the continuation of the society.

She was tireless in her work, receiving and replying to hundreds of letters every week for several years after her second book was published. She replied personally to every letter, in ink, and would often stay up to the early hours to finish her work. I have seen a couple of her letters and can vouch for the personal touch and thought she put into them.

It is believed that in 1963 Miss Bruce's health began to deteriorate with the failure of her eyesight and possible development of Alzheimer's disease. Mrs. P, her maid, did her best to cope but it was too much work trying to look after Miss Bruce who became confined to her bed. Miss Bruce spent the last 12 months of her life in a nursing home in Cheltenham. She died on November 25th 1964, the causes of death synonymous with old age and poor mental health, and was cremated at Cheltenham cemetery, with many people turning up at her funeral. There was no plaque to commemorate Miss Bruce but there is an entry into the book of remembrance

Miss Bruce inoculating a compost heap with Q.R. activator.

which reads; "Passed into greater light and fuller service 1964". I suspect that the entry was submitted by her twin sisters Netty and Norah.

Lady Eve Balfour wrote her obituary in the Spring 1965 edition of *Mother Earth*, finalising the article as follows; 'The Soil Association cannot help but be the poorer for the absence of the driving force of her personality with its unswerving spirit-guided integrity of purpose, and everyone who met her, for however a short time, will feel they have lost a friend. But those who were privileged to know her well, will have no doubt at all that she is still working as hard as ever for the ideals to which she devoted her time on earth, and that she is still near and helping us to do likewise.'

Miss Bruce was responsible for introducing more than 400 new members to the Soil Association which was a remarkable achievement. Probably even more outstanding is the countless thousands of people all over the world, over the many years that her method was popular and to this day, who have been influenced by Miss Bruce's work; encouraging them to take up composting, adding to the life and health of the soil and in turn to the health of plants and animals on our planet. With her incredible achievements in mind, we can stand back, be forever thankful to Miss Bruce for what she gave to the world, and declare that in her days on this earth she made great strides towards the fulfilment of her main ambition in life, in essence; 'Give back Life to the soil, and thus eventually abolishing disease in plant, animal and man.'

The towering valerian (on the left) and lustrous blue delphiniums grown in the borders mulched with Q.R. Compost.

CHAPTER 2

The 'Q.R. Sustainable Organic Garden'

Before we delve into sustainability and all those clever sorts of words, we must first ask a very basic question; 'Why do we make compost?' It seems like an obvious question and my guess is that if you're reading this book then you shouldn't really need too much convincing that composting is a good idea. Having said that, awareness to why we should make compost becomes even more apparent the more you indulge. It is a reciprocating relationship; the more you do it, the more you learn about it and the more you learn about it the easier it gets, in fact I think it is one of those subjects in which you never stop learning, making it both very interesting and magnetic. As yet, I have found no drawbacks, no disadvantages, no insurmountable problems, and no good reasons for not doing it. But be warned - it is contagious and addictive!

Spinach and onions growing happily in the Q.R. compost fed soil; irrigation from mains supplied water is kept to a minimum, slugs take just the odd nibble on the spinach (pest controls are not employed).

The following are some good reasons why we should make compost and is by no means exhaustive:

Somewhere between 20% and 50% of household waste is compostable. Making compost at home turns a liability into an asset. The government have set targets to recycle or compost 30% of household waste by 2010. Why should you let them have it? It's your waste, you've paid for it and so you deserve to get the benefits from it!

Using compost, which is very dark in colour, as an addition to the soil, darkens the colour of the soil. Clay soils for example, which can be naturally pale grey or light brown in colour become very dark with the addition of plenty of humus. This enables the soil to warm up quicker and acts like a heat sink particularly under glass where short wave radiation is allowed through the glass and is absorbed by the soil as heat but longer wave radiation reflected back from the soil is trapped. This is particularly beneficial when using cloches or in the greenhouse. This theory was exploited by Jocelyn Chase who knew that this would mean quicker germination and would benefit root development (see Chapter 9). For soils that are already dark brown in colour, the difference may not be so apparent but there should an improvement to some degree in absorption of heat.

Some people may think that composting is hard work; overall it actually saves on labour and time. The compost vastly improves the soils structure and drainage, little or no digging is required. When applied as mulch, where quantities permit, less weeding is required.

The health benefits of vegetables grown in good compost are astounding and have been studied and reported many times throughout the last century. Examples of this include the Hunza tribe of Northern India, who were studied by Robert McCarrison in the 1930's. They were a race of mountain people who were renowned for their robust health, longevity, happiness and wisdom. McCarrison's experiments at the Nutrition Research Laboratories at Coonoor in India proved that it was the food they ate and how it was grown that gave them their vigour. The conclusions of the experiment were that health-giving food can only be grown in fertile soil. The Hunza's practised their traditional and systematic method of making and using compost which produced the fertile soil and crops.

Adding compost to the soil improves the fertility and brings a greater diversity of microbes, insects and general wildlife to the garden. Pests are controlled by their natural predators in the eco system that is created. Plants are more healthy and immune to disease and resistant to attack from pests. There should be no need for introducing pest controls of any description.

Improvement of the water retentive capacity of soils and benefits lateral (horizontal) movement of water through soils, to plants undercover for example, which saves on watering. Jocelyn Chase was a firm believer in this theory, effectively eliminating the need to water directly under his cloches (see Chapter 9).

No toxic waste from composting. Anaerobic decomposition in landfill causes methane and toxic run off which contaminates soil and groundwater.

As an excellent hobby; it is a subject you can delve into and experiment with and take it as far as you like. It's a hobby you can do on your own doorstep (almost literally!) is inexpensive to set up and has an end product that is a valuable asset to the garden.

By adding compost to our soil, we improve the capability of the soil to hold onto and attract most nutrients in the soil rather than allowing them to leach away.

Lowering our personal carbon footprint is achieved by composting. For example if waste is composted at home then this removes the requirement for shipping it to municipal compost sites or landfill and saves on landfill space.

Environmentally, composting removes the requirement for fertilisers and peat. Some fertilisers whether they be non-organic fertilisers (nitrate of ammonia, superphospate etc.) or some organic fertilisers (fresh manure for instance) can potentially leach nutrients into water courses and drain systems. Ultimately this can end up in the sources for our water supplies and require costly process plant and equipment to remove them. A good composting process, such as the Q.R. method, will feed the soil without leaching.

Composting provides a means to move away from 'peat based' composts; peat bogs are rare, have unique flora and fauna, and act as 'carbon sinks' to mitigate the effects of climate change.

Composting and Sustainability

All the reasons listed previously are, in their own right, perfectly good incentives to make compost, but collectively, they have a purpose of paramount importance in that they aspire towards the major fulfilment of the *sustainable organic garden*. Almost unknowingly, making compost is a striving effort towards being sustainable. Sustainability is a difficult term to define and differs depending on who defines it. To keep it simple, I will define it as the ability of a system or process to perpetuate or maintain itself indefinitely without the assistance or intervention from an external source. It's still a bit of a mouthful but in terms of gardening this primarily implies:

- Self perpetuation in growing the flowers, herbs, vegetables and fruit as we desire.
- No imported compost or growing mediums such as peat.
- No imported fertilisers.
- No imported chemicals to assist with the activities in the garden.
- No consumption of imported fuel in maintaining the garden.
- No transportation of materials from the garden such as waste.

So by composting, as demonstrated in our list of reasons for composting, we are virtually there in terms of achieving a *sustainable organic garden*. There are some things such as mowing the lawn that will be very difficult for most people to turn into a sustainable practice and I'm fairly sure they don't want to keep a goat or a sheep in their back garden! Mowing the lawn does have an advantage though in that we reap the reward of the fertility from the grass and since freshly cut grass is a good heat producer in the compost heap, I won't lose any sleep over mowing the lawn.

Why Q.R. Compost Making is the Essence of the Sustainable Organic Garden

'There are many good ways to make compost
And one has just entered my head
If a man can't make compost when living
He can always make compost when dead!'

(Adaptation of an Irish limerick)

It follows on from our reasons for making compost listed previously that most methods of composting would satisfy the majority of requirements for achieving the *sustainable organic garden* and I do not wish to disparage any method of composting which can achieve this. For some people certain methods work and not so for others. Any form of organic composting has to be encouraged because ultimately they follow the ancient 'rule of return' and will all produce the same product – humus, the food of the soil.

This leads me to explain why Q.R. composting is of greater benefit than most other types of composting in achieving the *sustainable organic garden:*

- Q.R. composting is a total solution to the requirements of the *sustainable organic garden*. A fertility is created which is superior to many other methods of composting and with each cycle of composting the fertility of the garden increases. This in turn creates the balanced eco system necessary to counteract pests and diseases and necessary to obtain organic sustainability.

- Q.R. compost is a hot composting method which allows everything vegetative to be added to the heap including diseased plants, perennial weeds and their pernicious root systems and seed. At the very high temperatures which are reached and sustained, all of these will be killed off. Cold composting methods will not kill off seeds and pathogens and are therefore restrictive in their use.

- Q.R. compost can be made without the addition of manure to the heap whereas methods such as the Indore method require layers of fresh manure to be added which may not be readily available to most gardeners.

- Q.R. compost achieves excellent results for the flower and vegetable garden. There are numerous testaments to the benefits of the method and the quality of the compost referred to in her books. For example, Lady Eve Balfour, the founder of the Soil Association was a keen follower of Miss Bruce's Q.R. method and carried out an experiment at the Haughley Research Station proving its worth beyond any doubt when used on the farm (see Chapter 1).

- Q.R. compost has everything the soil needs. The vitality from the flowers that are used in the activator is passed onto the plants through the soil making them healthy. Whatever a soil lacks it can provide. If the activator is made from herbs grown in the garden, the roots of the herbs will reach down into the depths of the subsoil to obtain the nutrients that the top soil may lack and in turn these nutrients will be passed on into the garden soil through the compost made with this activator.

- Q.R. composting is a practical, efficient and successful method for *all* types of gardens and gardeners.

- Q.R. compost requires no turning, saving time, effort and use of machinery for large scale operations.

The underlying principal behind the *'Q.R. Sustainable Organic Garden'* is that there is a natural cycling of materials in a virtually continuous 'closed loop' system. This means that there is very little need for the input of materials to the system from the outside world and also there is no need for removal of waste materials from the system to the outside world. Even the herbs that are used in the activator are grown in the garden, almost sensing what the soil lacks, searching out those minerals from deep down in the subsoil and adding them into the system. The diagram of the system at the end of the chapter shows the processing of everyday vegetative waste materials from the house and garden. This process takes all these waste materials through the Q.R. compost heap which is central to the whole eco system, quickly turning them with relatively low labour input, into a commodity that literally feeds the whole garden. Quite simply, this 'food', along with freely available sunlight and rainwater provides everything that is necessary for the sustenance of the garden. Everywhere the compost is applied will result in plants of exceptional health and vitality, even wild flowers and herbs will be stronger and bigger. The valerian I grow in the garden for making the Q.R. activator reached 2.4m high and had to be supported, whereas in the wild it generally grows to about 1.5m high. The colours of the flowers in the garden are more intense and the flowers last longer; previously, the flowers on my delphiniums would be over and done with in a couple of weeks, however, after applying the compost as a mulch around them last year, they flourished for almost six weeks and were of an amazingly deep, lustrous blue. Whilst I have still to exploit the full benefits of the compost in the vegetable plot, I have had overwhelming results from vegetables such as broccoli and parsnips which were much larger and tastier than anything I have bought in the shops and had no problems from pests and disease. The result of all this healthy produce is that a fair proportion of it, along with all the other vegetative waste from the garden, ends up back in the compost heap thus adding its vitality and fertility back into the system, accumulating with each cycle that is made and over the years building up the health and fertility of the garden as a whole.

Obviously, the more you can achieve towards the total sustainability goal, the better, but the diagram is idealistic and there may well be many factors influencing people's lives that will affect their ability to achieve total sustainability in the gardening process. For example, these could be things like not having enough time available to make the Q.R. compost activator which would have to be purchased from a supplier or additional watering from mains supplied water if plants can only be grown in containers. Also, it may not be possible to grow your own fruit and vegetables because of lack of space and these will have to be purchased elsewhere but if the impact can be lowered by purchasing locally grown seasonal vegetables (and ideally organic) then all the better. Certain activities also require machinery which in turn requires fuel, such as cutting the hedge, shredding the hedge clippings and mowing the lawn. These are factors that require some external influence outside the garden but they are not detrimental to the process; the main objective is to simply establish the compost heap as the hub of a cyclic system with three major parts; firstly the processing of vegetative waste in the Q.R. compost bin, secondly application of the compost to the garden and finally returning the waste materials from the house and garden back to the compost heap. The following chapters will help you to create this vital process.

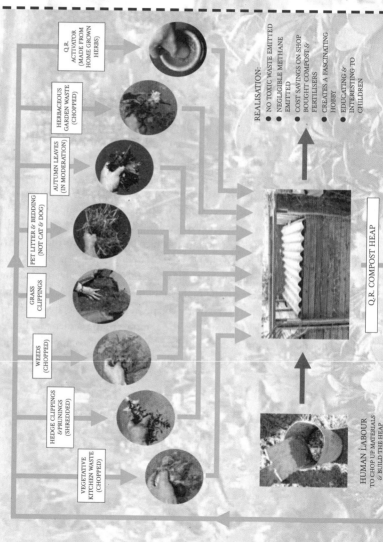

MATERIALS GENERATED & ACTIVITIES CARRIED OUT WITHIN THE GARDEN ZONE

VEGETATIVE KITCHEN WASTE (CHOPPED)

HEDGE CLIPPINGS & PRUNINGS (SHREDDED)

WEEDS (CHOPPED)

GRASS CLIPPINGS

PET LITTER & BEDDING (NOT CAT & DOG)

AUTUMN LEAVES (IN MODERATION)

HERBACEOUS GARDEN WASTE (CHOPPED)

Q.R. ACTIVATOR (MADE FROM HOME GROWN HERBS)

REALISATION:
- NO TOXIC WASTE EMITTED
- NEGLIGIBLE METHANE EMITTED
- COST SAVINGS ON SHOP BOUGHT COMPOST & FERTILISERS
- CREATES A FASCINATING HOBBY
- EDUCATING & INTERESTING TO CHILDREN

Q.R. COMPOST HEAP

HUMAN LABOUR
TO CHOP UP MATERIALS & BUILD THE HEAP

'THE Q.R. SUSTAINABLE ORGANIC GARDEN'

SEEDS
HARVESTED FROM PLANTS GROWN IN THE GARDEN

Q.R. COMPOST

THE GARDEN SOIL

SUNLIGHT

ACCUMULATING FERTILITY

HEALTHY HERBS, FLOWERS, FRUIT, TREES, VEGETABLES, GRASS & WEEDS

NATURAL WATERING
BY RAINFALL PLUS COLLECTION IN WATER BUTTS AND IRRIGATION USING SOAKER HOSE

REALISATION:
- NO DIGGING REQUIRED
- DARKENS THE SOIL SO WARMS UP QUICKLY ENCOURAGING PLANT GROWTH & EXTENDS GROWING SEASON
- GREATER DIVERSITY OF WILDLIFE
- BALANCED ECOSYSTEM RESULTING IN FEWER PESTS
- INCREASED MOISTURE RETENTION OF SOIL - SAVES WATER
- LESS WEEDING WHEN THE COMPOST IS USED AS A MULCH
- IMPROVED ATTRACTION & RETENTION OF NUTRIENTS WITHIN THE SOIL
- IMPROVED SOIL STRUCTURE

REALISATION:
- HEALTHIER PEOPLE & ANIMALS (PETS)
- COST SAVINGS ON SHOP BOUGHT PRODUCE
- ZERO FOOD MILES
- LESS MEDICAL INTERVENTION & MEDICAL COSTS

'THE OUTSIDE WORLD'

REALISATION:
- NO EXPORTATION OF WASTE FROM THE GARDEN
- NO IMPORTATION OF FERTILISERS, PEST CONTROL & GROWING MEDIA
- MINIMAL WATERING BY MAINS SUPPLIED WATER
- LOW CARBON FOOTPRINT
- SUSTAINABILITY

CHAPTER 3

The Theories Behind The Compost Heap and The Activator

If we can obtain an understanding of how a compost heap works, then we can take this knowledge and implement it to build compost heaps that will work effectively, efficiently and with the minimum of effort in the production of compost with a good manurial value. This may seem a distant goal to people who have little or no experience of composting and for people who have had bad composting experiences, but once an understanding of the living processes, dietary needs and habitats of the living creatures within the compost is obtained, the door to making good compost is opened. It's a bit like keeping pets; if you don't look after them properly they could become ill and possibly die, but if you nurture them and cater for their dietary and environmental needs they will reward you with good health and longer life. For example, if we attempted to feed a cat only on grass it would probably starve to death or if a dog was given plant nutrients then it would possibly be poisoned or starved. Similarly, if a creature, such as ourselves, is submerged in water then we will drown or if a fish is taken out of water it will die. Obviously we are quoting extremes here but the point is that if we can provide and optimise the environmental and dietary needs of the inhabitants of the heap, then we can create and support a healthy and balanced eco system for the production of nutrient rich compost.

The next two sections in this chapter deal firstly with the theory of how the compost heap works and subsequently how the activator works and from these descriptions we will be able to define the environmental and dietary conditions that the compost heap requires in order to make it successful.

How the Compost Heap Works

A good compost heap is not intended to be a rubbish dump where you can get rid of your refuse, it is an 'engineered' environment or home, designed to provide food, air, moisture and shelter for what I term the 'compost-makers' to carry out their work. The main 'compost-makers' are bacteria, fungi, protozoa, nematodes, arthropods, worms and gastropods. The following descriptions of the 'compost-makers' relate to their dietary and environmental requirements, activities and life processes from the main viewpoint of the roles they play in making the compost. These processes and activities are mainly those that happen in normal healthy soil and are generally associated with a 'soil food web', as defined and detailed in the book, 'Teaming with Microbes' by Jeff Lowenfels and Wayne Lewis. This web is a fierce world of prey and predator, life and death, and 'dog eat dog' which primarily establishes the precious foundations of many of the food chains from which our own food is sourced. In essence, the compost heap is really a refined and tuned version of what goes on in the soil.

Bacteria   These are the smallest and most abundant micro-organisms in the heap, munching away at the fresh and rotting vegetation. Bacteria are most prevalent where there is a presence of fresh green vegetative material because they are more succesful than the other 'compost-makers' at breaking down the simple sugars which are present in these materials. For most bacteria, the main requirement of their diet is carbon, which gives them the energy they require for their metabolic activity. Nitrogen is also required for two reasons; firstly, to help them produce enzymes that break down their food and secondly; to form amino acids that are required in the production of their cell structures. In consuming these nutrients, they become tied up inside the bodies of the bacteria and are only released when the bacteria die or are eaten by a predator such as a nematode that will digest and excrete the waste products. In turn the nematode will be eaten, digested and waste products excreted by its predators again releasing nutrients available for plant uptake.

Initially, bacteria fall into two categories, aerobic and anaerobic. The aerobic bacteria are normally considered to be beneficial, requiring air to 'breathe' and breaking down material to a sweet smelling consistency. The anaerobic bacteria can exist in airless conditions and are generally associated with bad smells and putrefaction. For example, the smell of bad eggs (hydrogen sulphide) is a result of anaerobic bacteria producing sulphurous waste. Anaerobic conditions, such as compaction causing exclusion of air, can encourage pathogenic bacteria which can kill off beneficial aerobic bacteria, as well as causing diseases, so these conditions must be avoided. In defence, good bacteria in aerobic conditions, can produce antibiotics which can eradicate bad bacteria.

Bacteria also fall into 3 other categories dependent upon the temperature conditions in which they thrive best. The question that has always intrigued me the most about hot composting is where does the heat come from? The answer is that it is the release of energy as heat from the result of the high metabolic activity of the bacteria themselves. In a single teaspoon of compost there will be billions of bacteria, and under the right conditions, these will be busy producing enzymes, absorbing materials, digesting, excreting and reproducing, which they do mainly by cell division, hence there is lots of activity and heat produced. Under the right conditions a single bacteria can produce millions of offspring within hours.

There are bacteria that can exist at sub zero temperatures, even in places as cold as the Antarctic. In the compost heap the bacterial activity starts at about 13° C by bacteria known as psychrophilic bacteria; their name is Greek in origin and is derived from the words *'psukhros'* meaning 'cold' and *philos* meaning 'loving'. As they start to digest food they will increase the temperature, then reproduce causing further increase in temperature, until the temperature reaches approximately 20° C which is when the psychrophilic bacteria will die off and mesophilic (from Greek *mesos* meaning 'intermediate') bacteria will take over. These are very efficient decomposers and work alongside fungi, worms and insects in the breaking down of the compost. Again the temperature continues to increase if conditions are favourable until temperatures reach approximately 40°C and then thermophilic (from Greek *thermos* meaning 'hot') bacteria take over. These bacteria can exist in high temperatures up to approximately 70°C and can break down complex carbohydrates such as hemicelluloses. A period of a few days at approximately 65°C is beneficial to the heap since at these temperatures for this duration, pathogens are killed off and weed seeds and roots are destroyed. It is desirable not to let temperatures within the heap increase much above 65°C because at these temperatures many microbes cannot survive and valuable carbon can be burnt off. When temperatures reach these levels, many bacteria and fungi are killed off along with any creatures that cannot mobilise themselves sufficiently to retreat to cooler parts of the heap, such as nematodes. Some bacteria can survive periods of environmental stress, such as high temperature, by producing a special dormant cell called an endospore which has a coating that is resistant to many extremes, chemicals and toxins. However, there are many survivors at the outer, cooler parts of the heap ready to recolonise the heap when it cools and bacteria such as Actinomyctes take over. These are bacteria that can form filaments or chains which resemble fungi and are instrumental in the final breaking down of tough components that linger in the heap such as cellulose, chitin, lignin and proteins. Actinomyctes are responsible for the sweet earthy smell emitted from good compost.

Bacteria differ to fungi in their dietary requirements and therefore these two types of organism can work together side by side in the decomposition process. Most bacteria like to feed on the more basic, simpler materials that are easier to digest but some bacteria can also break down complex chains of molecules containing carbon, reducing them to simple sugars, amino acids and fatty acids which are the essential requirements for bacteria to survive. The fungi are left to deal with the harder materials that bacteria cannot cope with which include substances such as cellulose and lignin (a very tough material that binds and protects cellulose), however, bacteria can also finish off the work that fungi start.

To allow them to adhere to surfaces and prevent them being washed away, bacteria produce a slime. This slime is slightly alkaline in its nature and therefore by adding lots of fresh green vegetative material (high in nitrogen content) to the compost heap, which attract bacteria, the compost produced will be more alkaline in nature than a heap that is built from mainly woody materials (high in carbon content).

Bacteria require moisture in which to carry out their work; it is a pre-requisite to allow them to take up nutrients and release waste products and it allows them to travel to find food. Without moisture they go into dormancy.

Fungi It may be surprising to learn that fungi carry out the major work of decomposition in the compost heap. They have the capability to penetrate and break down hard substances such as cellulose and lignin and create a gateway for bacteria to enter. Fungi produce very powerful enzymes that allow them to penetrate tough material including proteins by breaking down the bonds in materials which hold the nutrients in place within the material. These enzymes are very acidic and contribute to the acidic nature of a compost heap if it is built from mainly carbon type materials.

By introducing soil into the compost heap (a shovelful at each layer is recommended) we introduce the microbes, including fungi that are present in the soil and will exist when the compost returns to the soil. In normal soil conditions (outside the compost heap), these fungi, with their probing hyphae (the long thin strands that fungi send out), can extend over several metres and transport nutrients to plants in exchange for proteins and carbohydrates. In the heap there is no living plant material (or shouldn't be!) and therefore the nutrients are tied up within the fungi until it dies or until it comes into contact with a plant that it is attracted to when the compost is added to the soil. When the fungi dies it will be consumed by other 'compost-makers' and will leave behind a network of air passages that will help anaerobic bacteria to breathe and allow water to flow and drain through the compost.

As a fungus extends and moves through the compost, it leaves behind a trail of excess acids and enzymes which will continue the digestion of organic materials after the fungus has moved away. Fungi can bridge air gaps in materials and therefore do not have the same moisture requirements as bacteria. Fungi can be attracted into the compost heap by the addition of food materials such as bran and oats. As an experiment, if you place a small heap of these on the soil, as the material picks up moisture you will see a furry white fungal growth engulf the pile which will quickly rot down and disappear within a few weeks.

Protozoa means 'first animal' and these are single celled organisms, considered to be the smallest of all animals. There are three main types of protozoa, namely amoebas, flagellates, and ciliates. They mainly live in wet or moist conditions and are very mobile, feeding mostly on bacteria and themselves. When protozoa feed on bacteria, the majority of the nitrogen that is consumed by and tied up in bacteria, is released as nitrogen available for plants, since the protozoa do not need so much for their life processes.

Amoebae are able to shape shift, which they use for propulsion as well as catching their prey (bacteria and other protozoa) by surrounding them, quite quickly if necessary. Flagellates have short, whip-like tails (a bit like a tadpole) which propel them through the wet conditions they prefer. Protozoa feed by taking in water through their porous membranes; the water containing bacteria for food and oxygen to breathe. The by-products from the protozoa are carbon dioxide, nitrogen and other nutrients which are released in water and exit through the membrane.

Along with nematodes, Protozoa consume the bacteria and fungi which have tied up all the nutrients from the food (rotting vegetation in the compost heap). When the bacteria and fungi are consumed the nutrients within them are released in the excrement of the predator. This process is called mineralisation. It is absolutely essential that healthy populations of protozoa and nematodes are present in the soil to ensure mineralisation occurs when compost is applied to the soil. It almost goes without saying that pesticides and chemicals may destroy these creatures which in turn will inhibit this process and will restrict the availability of nutrients for uptake by plants.

Nematodes Nematodes are blind, non segmented round worms that can exist in almost any habitat and their name comes from the Latin *nema* meaning 'thread'. They are predatory upon bacteria, fungi, algae, yeasts and small invertebrates including other nematodes. They can also be parasitic upon invertebrate and vertebrate hosts such as large animals including man. Plants can also come under attack from nematodes and in this respect much research has been carried out by scientists in efforts to combat them. Nematodes can be beneficial predators of grubs, wasps and weevils and invertebrates such as slugs; a biological control method for slugs uses these nematodes. Nematodes in soils and compost can range in size from approximately 0.25mm to 5.5mm long and usually, cannot be seen with the naked eye. Many microbes, including nematodes can be killed off by the intense heat of the compost, but usually enough survive around the edges of the heap and when they do so there are abundant food supplies for them to re-colonise the heap and thrive.

Nematodes are essential for the mineralisation of nutrients, as discussed previously, and since they require relatively low amounts of nitrogen for their upkeep, they are able to release large amounts of nitrogen for plant uptake.

It is known that nematodes search for food by various mechanisms including heat or chemical detection. In the warm conditions of the compost heap, associated with the metabolic activity of the bacteria, the nematode will home in on the particular temperature it associates with the abundance of food. It can also follow chemical messages though this may be to its detriment since some parasitic fungi emit chemicals to attract nematodes. This can be a distinct advantage to the organic gardener if the nematode is an undesirable type that feeds on plants and causes diseases within them.

Arthropods consist of invertebrates such as centipedes, millipedes, woodlice, beetles, spiders etc. Approximately 75% of all animals are arthropods and as a result they dominate the animal kingdom. In terms of composting, their main role is in shredding material whereby they chew up fresh and decomposing material, making it into smaller pieces, creating more surface areas allowing bacteria and fungi to enter into materials and generally speeding up the decomposition process. Some species also feed on bacteria and fungi and hence release substantial amounts of nutrient in their excrement. Arthropods are also much more mobile than fungi or bacteria and can transport spores and bacteria, taking them to areas rich in food. In hot composting, arthropods generally come into the heap when it starts to cool off; they will feed upon the bacteria, fungi, protozoa, nematodes and worms causing their populations to increase; they will forage, aerate, shred and open up the materials allowing bacteria and fungi to penetrate further; they have a role to play which is as vital to the production of compost as any of the other 'compost-makers'.

Worms Singularly, worms are probably the most important animals in the compost heap. I say singularly because it is possible to make compost using worms alone (well almost alone; they have bacteria in their stomachs which digest food for them) in a worm bin.

Generally, the main type of worm entering the compost bin is the brandling or tiger worm (Eisenia Foetida) which is reddish with yellow stripes (segments) and can grow up to about 15cm in length. Brandling worms feed mainly upon organic matter, unlike the earthworm which feeds mainly on bacteria, and are only found in soils that have relatively high concentrations of organic matter. They favour temperatures between 12 and 25°C and moisture levels approaching 75% and under these conditions, given the right sort of food, they will reproduce quickly. Worms are hermaphrodites and carry the sexual organs of both sexes but it still takes two worms to 'tango' and produce offspring! The worm has a slime tube where it incubates the worm eggs which are encased in small cocoons, the small lemon shaped structures which can be found in the compost. When the eggs hatch there will be at least 15 thread like baby worms in each cocoon. These babies grow quickly, reaching sexual maturity in approximately 4 to 6 weeks and populations can double within a month.

Worms do not have any teeth, instead they have a strong muscle part way down their digestive tract called the gizzard which contains sand and rock particles specifically for the purpose of grinding up food. This breaks the food down into smaller particles and opens it up ready to be digested by bacteria in the intestines. Before the food enters the intestine it is coated with liquefied calcium carbonate (limestone). The bacteria in the intestine can then digest the food to produce nutrients which are absorbed into the worm's bloodstream through the walls of the intestine. Excess organic matter is excreted out of the worm as a worm cast. For plants, the wormcast is like a 5 star Michelin chef dinner; in comparison to soil that hasn't passed though a worm, vermicastings typically contain significant increases in the quantities of nitrogen, phosphorous, potassium magnesium and calcium. The vermicasts are extremely rich in organic matter and therefore have a high C.E.C. (cation exchange capacity) which basically means they hold a large amount of negatively charged particles which attract the positively charged particles of many nutrients. This allows them to hold onto many nutrients, though not all since some have positive charges such as potassium and nitrates and these can be readily washed out of the soil.

Worms are excellent at shredding; reducing and breaking down the vegetative matter that is added to the compost heap. Their action allows bacteria and fungi easier access and to gain footholds in tough materials such as lignin and cellulose. They also reduce the organic matter into tiny particles that other microbes can readily consume and therefore, they greatly speed up the decomposition of organic materials. Worms are effective travellers through soil and compost, creating airways, mixing materials, transporting bacteria and fungi to new places where there is food and also depositing more food in these places with their castings. Worms can move both horizontally and vertically in soil leaving tunnels which provide drainage and aid in the lateral movement of water through the soil which is of particular benefit to cloche gardening. These tunnels can also provide passages in the soil for roots to penetrate. The humus created by worms increases the water retentive capabilities of the compost or soil into which it is added. All these qualities make the worm invaluable in the making of compost and of massive benefit to any soils in particular those to which compost is added.

Snails and Slugs are part of the order of molluscs and are residents in most people's gardens, perhaps considered as a pest by many; eating their way through the lush and juicy leaf matter of our prized vegetables and flowers as well as the odd bit of fruit for pudding. Like all creatures they have a place in this world and in a balanced eco system they should not be such a problem to gardeners. There are plenty of natural predators for these creatures, such as beetles, spiders, snakes, frogs, hedgehogs and birds. All we need to do is to allow or help the right conditions to exist to attract these predators such as building a pond for frogs and toads to colonise or providing piles of logs to shelter hedgehogs. When the fertility of a garden is increased by the regular addition of compost, the diversity of creatures starts to increase and with this comes the rewards of allowing Mother Nature's ways to deal with pests. My motto is 'live and let live'. When molluscs venture into compost heaps, usually at the edges where it is cool or when the heap has cooled off, they actually become very useful in breaking down organic matter. Like worms, they are experts at shredding and happily exist beneath the soil (or compost) surface which is where they spend most of their time. This is where they are providing benefit to gardeners in shredding organic matter, breaking it open and creating access for bacteria and fungi to do their work. They are equipped with a tooth covered tongue called a radula, which is used like a rasp to grate food. When they move around on their 'eating foot' (translation of gastro pod) they secrete slime which is made from protein and sugars. This slime helps to bind particles of soil together and increases its water retention properties. In their burrowing activities they provide the same advantages as worms such as improving drainage and allowing root penetration in soils.

How the Activator Works

I believe the role of the activator is to work in harmony with the creatures in the compost heap, reinforcing their vitality, giving them what they lack and creating maximum health. Good compost is not about a load of nutrients ready for plants to eat. If you only want to give them nutrients then chemicals can do this, but there will be no life in the soil since the salts in the chemicals will drive away or destroy this life. Once the chemicals and any humus are used up there is nothing left and soil structure and health in the soil and subsequently in the plants will suffer. Good compost contains the life (the microbes) with the vitality to cycle the nutrients and minerals and keep on cycling them provided there is food available for the microbes. Good compost is considerate of what is to come, not to give instant gratification. Good compost and good soil are full of life!

In Miss Bruce's day there was a considerable understanding of the action and role of the 'compost-makers' (defined in the section above) and the processes involved in decomposition, however, in her books Miss Bruce did not discuss this in any great detail, probably because there was the presence of other literature at the time such as the 'Living Soil' by Lady Eve Balfour and 'Compost' by F. H. Billington which covered this topic and which are made reference to within Miss Bruce's books.

Miss Bruce described her two main beliefs or 'convictions' as she called them, quoted from her book 'From Vegetable Waste to Fertile Soil', as follows:

1. 'That all growth is the interplay of living forces – not the result of automatic chemical change. That these forces pass through the soil, permeate atmosphere, are carried by the elements, and are behind the mystery, the vitality of plant growth. With quick and controlled disintegration these living forces are released and radiate into the heap. There they work in vast co-operation with the fungi, bacteria, earthworms, and other soil workers, and are returned to the earth strengthened by the herbal essences, ready for use once again for plants and in the same rhythm of life as the plants

themselves.'

2. 'There is life throughout the universe – life, manifesting at a different rhythm in each of the four kingdoms.'

Miss Bruce's theory is hinged upon the rhythm of life within the compost being in sympathy with or in the same 'rhythm' as that of the soil to which it would be added, there being different 'rhythms' for the mineral, vegetable, animal and human kingdoms. If constituents of differing kingdoms, such as mineral salts or blood are added to the soil then they unbalance the rhythm of life in the soil and weaken its constitution. Fresh manure is unpalatable to the soil and burns plants because of the digestive juices it contains, however, well rotted manure is one of the finest forms of humus since these juices are no longer present.

Miss Bruce proclaimed that the Q.R. activator worked on the principles of radiations or vibrations that emanate from the energies and life within the solutions which when added to the heap radiate through it imparting their energies and life to the content. The minute quantities of the flower essences within the solutions mean that these energies are confined within the heap and hence adding too little or too much would mean that the Q.R. process could fail to work. The flower essences capture the 'living forces' or 'divine' energy within the flower which pass on their energies to the contents of the heap, as summed up by Miss Bruce's inspired words "The divinity within the flower is sufficient in itself". It is partly the careful handling, storage and application of this energy to the compost heap that ensures its success. The other procedures that make it successful come with the understanding of how the radiations work. For the radiations to travel through the heap, they need a moist media (but without the expulsion of air). Hence Miss Bruce advised that material should be packed quite tightly to ensure there were no large air gaps. When adding layers of material, this was achieved by gently packing the materials from the outside edge, working towards the centre of the heap. As the composting process gets under way, the soft green materials are digested quickly and therefore air pockets are created and hence she also advised light treading after the addition of a few layers to close the gaps back up. It is also important that air can still circulate through the heap to allow microbes to breathe therefore compaction should be avoided. (Miss Bruce described the heap as being alive and therefore it needs to breathe). The fact that the energies are required to stay within the heap means holding on to the heat as much as possible and preventing the energies escaping. This is ensured by covering the heap by placing a layer of sacking over the top of the compost to retain heat. The open weave of the sack also allows the heap to breathe.

Miss Bruce's theory was probably quite a lot for some people to take in, but she had the gift of being able to present her ideas without being labelled as a crank with thousands of people all over the world using her method and with many still doing so today. In my own experience, I have attempted to persuade relatives, friends, colleagues, neighbours etc. and have been met with certain disbelief that such a small amount of powder can have the capability to produce good compost. The natural urge is to put more in the heap than is required, possibly in the thinking that it will work even better. In effect the opposite will happen.

Science and technology have advanced vastly since Miss Bruce's day and the concepts she put forward may seem even harder to swallow now that we have more and more scientific research providing evidence to prove or disprove theories. There is one theory, however, that science will find practically impossible to unravel and that is the age old question of 'the meaning of life', as explained in Miss Bruce's words "Yet there is life in all that exists, and what is life? Do we not find the answer in the words of the Eastern sage as he writes of: 'The divinity that sleeps in the stones, stirs in the plants, wakes in the animals, is conscious alone in man'. The breath of God in all that is. *That* is life."

Who is this 'Eastern Sage' Miss Bruce refers to? Some quick research on the internet revealed that the proverb is an ancient one of the Sufi philosopher, Ibn Al'arabi. Perhaps 'the Sage' is inferring that man does not simply exist, he has the 'gift' of self awareness and capacity to realise that life is more than just flesh and blood, that there is a life force that is divinely created that cannot be destroyed, which will move on after the body has expired? The same therefore exists in the other kingdoms without this self awareness? Is it the same divinity or living force that is shared by all four kingdoms, have they just got different rhythms set by their level of awakening?

Whether or not one has a view on the metaphysical aspects of Q.R. compost making, the main point is that the method works and has been proven to do so for over sixty years.

Key Conditions
for the Correct Dietary Needs & Environment for
Q.R. Composting

In many respects, the ideal compost heap has the pre-requisites for living desired by many creatures, it provides, food, air, water, and shelter for its inhabitants. It really is *common sense,* as Miss Bruce would say. In providing these conditions, the stage is set for the establishment of a 'soil food web' that will continue to grow and develop, increasing in its fertility and then continuing the process when the compost is added to the soil. The 'compost-makers' will continue to do their work in the soil, reproducing and inoculating the soil, distributing the humus and combining it with the existing soil to improve structure and converting nutrients tied up in themselves into plant available nutrients. As is so for the compost heap, it is important that there are no pesticides, fungicides, herbicides or artificial fertilisers present in the soil when the compost is added otherwise members of, or all of, the food web will be destroyed and the good work will be wasted. The nutrients in the compost itself will be available but the soil will be lifeless and the fertility short lived.

The following requirements are all essential to the well being of the heap:

Food; The correct choice and balance of 'greens' and 'browns' (see Chapter 5 for definitions) is required to determine the outcome of the quality and ph of the compost. Put rubbish in and you will get rubbish out. Add *good food such as fresh green weeds full of vitality* and this vitality will be passed on to the final compost.

Air; is crucial for the living processes such as breathing of aerobic organisms including bacteria. *Light compaction* is best. Heavy compaction should be avoided to ensure that anaerobic conditions do not exist.

Moisture; is required for the movement of bacteria and many protozoa, and is favourable to worms. Bacteria also require it for the uptake of nutrients and release of waste products. Moisture is also essential for the energies of the flower essences to permeate through the compost. *Ideal humidity is about 50%.* Obviously this is not easy to monitor unless you have a humidity meter rigged up to the heap. Experience is the key to getting this right. When adding 'brown' materials (see Chapter 5) ensure that they are suitably moisturised before adding them to the heap.

Siting the bin directly on soil and providing drainage ensures that the heap does not become saturated, thus avoiding anaerobic conditions. Do not site the bin at the bottom of a slope for the same reasons you wouldn't pitch a tent there!

Shelter; is imperative to maintain correct moisture levels within the heap, to avoid both evaporation and drenching. *A roof or rainproof cover* over your compost bin is essential.

Insulation; Essential to prevent the loss of heat and subsequent decline in the disintegration process. In the Q.R. composting method, this is usually provided by a *layer of sacking.*

Soil; The introduction of a spade full of soil at each layer *introduces the 'compost-makers'* to the heap which include the right types of bacteria, fungi, protozoa, nematodes, worms etc. that are essential to the process. *Also by siting the bin directly on soil* allows these microbes to enter the heap and provides somewhere to retreat to if conditions are unsuitable.

Lime; aids in the conversion of ammonia to nitrates and also reduces the acidity of the heap. It is beneficial for the digestive processes of worms as grit for their gizzard and acts as source of calcium carbonate for coating food ready for digestion. *A light sprinkling of crushed limestone* at intervals of a few layers is sufficient.

(Please refer to Chapter 5 for further details on providing dietary requirements. Chapter 6 supplies the method for provision of all the environmental requirements.)

The Primary Conditions for Q.R. Composting

From the key conditions previously listed we can derive four main conditions that must be complied with otherwise failure of the heap is inevitable:

1. Shelter.   2. Retention of heat.   3. Aeration.   4. Good drainage.

CHAPTER 4

Containing the Compost

In Miss Bruce's day, the Q.R. system was thoroughly proven with the traditional type compost bin. They were really the only type of bin available at that time and were easily made at home from timber posts and slats or in Miss Bruce's case railway sleepers. Today, the composter is spoilt for choice in which type of compost bin to use and it would be an almost impossible task to test them all with the Q.R. method. With this in mind, the main objective of this chapter is to relate to the composter the different types of bin that are known to successfully work with the Q.R. composting method.

Miss Bruce always encouraged experimentation and that is half the thrill of composting in that there is a certain elasticity in the method and it is adaptable to different conditions. There is no harm in trying the Q.R. method with any type of compost bin, as long as the four primary conditions of composting are met which are dealt with in Chapter 3, however, I suggest that the system may not work well with compost tumblers since I believe the frequent turning would work in opposition to the Q.R. composting process, disturbing the heap and disrupting the Q.R. compost making process. (See Q.R. activator theory explained in Chapter 3). After all, one of the main advantages of using the Q.R. method is that turning is not required. Furthermore compost tumblers do not allow beneficial insects and animals to enter the heap which would be a distinct disadvantage.

For the different types of bin described it is essential that they are used in conjunction with a layer of insulation material and it is advised that this should be in the form of a hessian sack, allowing the heap to breathe whilst retaining heat. Hessian sacks are still manufactured and can be obtained from seed suppliers as potato sacks. Old hessian sacks are ideal and are sometimes available from local 'freecycle' schemes.

As with all types of bin that are used with the Q.R. compost method, the time taken to build the heap must be no greater than 4 weeks. This can tie up the bin for a month

A range of compost bins showing the three main traditional type compost bins and various storage bins.

or two whilst the compost is maturing therefore additional bins are required for making or storing compost, no matter what the size of your garden.

The Traditional Bin

The traditional bin (or New Zealand bin as they are sometimes known) is generally made from timber slats fastened to a frame of timber posts with gaps between the slats to allow air to enter the heap. They work very well but need the addition of:

1. A rain cover to prevent rain water entering the heap and retarding or halting the compost process.

2. An insulation layer on top of the heap to retain the heat that is generated within the heap.

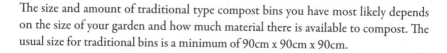

The size and amount of traditional type compost bins you have most likely depends on the size of your garden and how much material there is available to compost. The usual size for traditional bins is a minimum of 90cm x 90cm x 90cm.

Small gardens may be able to manage with a single bin which could be subdivided into two compartments (as explained in Chapter 6); one for building and one for maturing compost.

For medium to large gardens, ideally you will need at least 3 compost bins, the reason being that you will need one bin for building the current compost heap, one bin for a previously built maturing heap and one bin for storage and usage.

This type of bin is readily available from garden/horticultural suppliers such as Chase Organics, but it is also possible to make your own; I made mine from old pallets which helps the environment and has the additional benefit that they were free of charge.

Constructing a Traditional Bin from Pallets

The materials I used to make the bins are as follows:-

- 13 off Equal sized pallets, approx 1m x 1m
- 12 off 'L' brackets c/w 2 off 11mm diameter fixing holes
- 8 off M10 x 50mm hexagon nuts and bolts
- 4 off M10 x 75mm hexagon nuts and bolts
- 12 off timber battens 15mm x 25mm x 1m approx.
- 16 off 100mm x 12's woodscrews
- 2 off 40mm x 125mm x 3000mm timbers
- 3 off 1000mm x 1200mm heavy duty corrugated sheets
- 40mm nails as required
- 2 off Brushwood panels (1m x 1m)

Because pallets come in all shapes and sizes, the method I suggest is a fairly loose, non-detailed guide which is primarily intended to portray the main features that should be present in a home made traditional bin system. Some basic tools and DIY skills should be sufficient to construct these bins.

It is preferable if you can obtain all your pallets the same size so that they can easily be coupled together and make a regular shape when assembled. Ideally, the pallets should have sufficient air gaps of at least 1cm between the slats so that the heap can breathe.

As with all compost bins the traditional bins should be sited on bare soil or grass. The area in my garden where I chose to site the bins was previously a lawned area next to a post and wire fence with a briar rose shrub growing up against the fence. The rose bush was dug out as far as possible, but to ensure that the shrub and weeds on the other side of the fence did not return and grow in the bottom of the enclosures, a layer of breathable woven polyethylene landscape fabric was laid down underneath the entire area to be occupied by the bins, with an overlap of about 300mm all the way around. This does not appear to affect the entry and exit of creatures into the bin, however, the fabric can be removed after a couple of years when it is pretty certain that all roots have died back.

One of the main bins with the cover removed showing a compartmented bin. (Note the resting system for the cover support timbers and the 'L' bracket fixing the main partition to the rear wall)

The slats at the front of the bin are spaced apart using twigs to allow an air gap

When building the enclosures, I used pallets with the blocks and support timbers intact (as they come) for the two end panels and the three rear panels so that insulation material such as straw can be stuffed between the timbers to provide some insulation and keep wind-chill off the heap. If the heaps are situated in a very sheltered position or in a warm climate then this may not be necessary. I live in rural Northumberland and exposure to high winds is fairly frequent which can soon chill or dry out the sides of the heap. It is stressed here that everything must be done to maintain the heat within the heap whilst also allowing the heap to breathe.

The pallets for the two inner partitions were stripped of their support blocks and support timbers leaving a flat grid so that space is not wasted inside the enclosures. Bend over the sharp ends of the nails with a hammer so that they are not a future danger when working inside the bin.

I used 'L' shaped steel brackets to secure the sidewalls and partitions to the rear panels. The pallets were bolted in position using a bracket at the top and bottom of each sidewall/partition where it mates with the rear panel.

Before the front panels are fitted, it is necessary to obtain a long piece of stout timber, equal to the combined length of the three rear panels. This is screwed to the tops of the sidewalls and partitions at their front corners so that it holds the sidewalls and

A channel is provided to allow the slats to be removed or added.

partitions in place. A similar piece of timber is fitted along the front faces of the bottom corners of the sidewalls and partitions.

Removable wooden slats for the front panels are used to enable access whilst building the heaps. The slats should be no more than 10cm in height and should be about 1cm shorter in length than the width between the partitions/sidewalls so that they easily slide up and down. The slats are made from a few pallets which are stripped down to individual timbers. For each end of the slats, two battens are nailed in position to the sidewalls to create a channel for the slats to slide in. A 12cm gap should be left at the top of the battens to enable the slats to be added or removed. When the slats are slid into position they can be spaced apart to allow an air gap by inserting spacers between them at each end of the slat. Small stones or twigs make suitable spacers.

The two end panels and three rear panels are stuffed with straw in the gaps between the parallel sets of timber on each pallet, thus providing insulation for the heap. Because the two end panels are on show, they are covered with brushwood panelling (the type that comes on a roll) to neatly finish things off.

Heavy duty corrugated sheets were used for the rain covers. These are placed in position on top of wooden battens which rest on the front panel slats and a rear batten resting at an appropriate height between the gaps in the horizontal timbers of the sidewalls/partitions (see photograph on previous page). The rain covers do not protrude above the top of the bins but they are still weighted down with a couple of bricks to ensure that they don't blow away.

As with any sort of enclosure, heat retention for the Q.R. method is provided by sacking placed on top of the compost with the rain covers placed on top.

Whilst the home made enclosures took a fair amount of time and effort to build, they cost very little, suited my purposes exactly and I have found them to be very reliable, producing good compost within a couple of months.

Traditional Compost Bin
based on Miss Bruce's 'Plan for a Small Bin'

The following plan is an updated and modified version of that provided in Miss Bruce's book 'Common-Sense Compost Making' and can, in the main part, be constructed using timber from stripped down pallets:

Back uprights -7cm square x 135cm posts sunk into ground

Front boards loose for easy removal

Front uprights - 7cm square x 105cm posts sunk into ground

The slats at the front of the bin are spaced apart using twigs/bits of wood to allow an air gap

Size of compost bin depends on length of boards on pallets

Top board from pallet fixed to back uprights to provide platform to support corrugated roof

Air spaces

2 x uprights 7cm square x 90cm screwed to cross boards with a gap to allow front boards to easily drop in and out

posts sunk into ground

front, side and back boards made from stripped down pallets

Corrugated sheet weighted down to provide rainproof cover

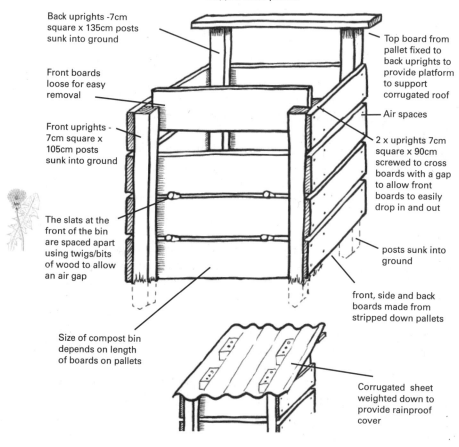

Traditional Bins Made From Railway Sleepers The bins that Miss Bruce used so successfully were constructed from railway sleepers. Miss Bruce did not give details of the construction method in her books, however, she did state that situating them adjacent to the stone walls in her garden allowed aeration of the compost due to the irregularities of the stones and the flat surface of the sleepers against them. Corrugated steel covers were used to keep out the rain and hessian sacks placed over the compost material to retain the heat. It is known that she subdivided her bins to suit her requirements, the smallest being no less than 60cm cubed. Using railway sleepers would provide good insulation for the heaps and prevent the edges of the heaps drying out. It is my intention to construct a set of bins using sleepers in the future and compare the results to those obtained from the traditional bins covered earlier in this chapter.

Cautionary Note: It is not recommended that railway sleepers treated with creosote or any other preservative are used for constructing compost bins. New or used untreated railway sleepers are available and suitable bins could be constructed from these.

The Quick Build Wire Netting Compost Bin

A plan for this type of bin was included in 'Common-Sense Compost Making'. It is a very useful bin because it is cheap to build and can be made in less than an hour, providing a temporary bin which can be very handy in such cases where all your bins may be full and you've got material that needs to be composted. I have used these on a couple of occasions and in terms of compost manufacture, I find that they work as well as the traditional type bins. They should be used in conjunction with a raincover and Hessian sacks as per the traditional compost bin. They can also be used as storage bins for materials waiting to be composted or for storing finished compost. I think that they are very adaptable and have an attractive rustic appearance which belies their low cost.

Constructing the Quick Build Wire Netting Compost Bin.
The materials required to construct this bin are:

- One piece of chicken wire measuring 0.9m x 8m (this usually comes in a 10m roll but it can easily be folded over to reduce it to the required length)

- One bale of straw or hay
- One stout rod or pole measuring approx 1.5m long (I used a reinforcing bar for concrete)
- One ball of nylon string
- 3 pieces of light timber approximately 1m long (planks off a pallet will do the job nicely)
- Corrugated sheet measuring 1m x 1m

Step 1 The chicken wire is laid out flat and then folded in half with the crease across its width. Open the netting back out and lay pieces of the straw or hay, approx 10cm thick, on top of the chicken wire until one half of the wire has been covered. Fold the chicken wire back over again so that the material is sandwiched between 2 layers of chicken wire.

Constructing a wire netting bin. *Step 1*

Step 2 Cut the string into pieces about 2m long and close up the open edges of the netting using an 'overlocking' type sewing action.

Step 3 The assembled sandwich should then be folded in half with a crease made across its width.

Step 4 Open the wire back out again and this time fold the 2 ends in so that they meet the fold in the middle and make firm creases where the folds are. There should now be four sections of equal size which will form the walls of the bin.

Step 2

Step 3

Step 4

Step 5 Position the assembly where it is required and manipulate the wire sandwich into the bin shape and stand it on one end.

Step 6 Locate the pole into one of the corners of the bin. Hammer the pole into the ground until it is firmly in place and secure the bin to the pole by tying it with string. Place an old drinking yoghurt pot or a similar plastic pot on top of the pole so that nobody can hurt themselves on it.

Step 7 The two ends of the sandwich are joined together with the string to finish the enclosure.

Step 8 Lay the 3 planks of wood across the top of the bin and place the corrugated sheet on top. A couple of bricks placed on top of the sheet will stop it blowing off in windy conditions.

Step 5

Step 6

Step 7

Step 8

The Green Line Garden Composter as available from Chase Organics.

Cuboid Plastic Bins

There are cuboid plastic types of bin which come complete with rain proof cover. I was informed by Mike Hedges of Chase Organics that he successfully uses this type of bin with the Q.R. compost method. This type of bin is available from Chase Organics as the Greenline Garden Composter. The method of extraction of the compost is from 2 large slide up doors at the bottom. Even for a small garden it is best that at least two of these bins are used so that the second bin can be filled while the first is maturing. As with all containers used for Q.R. compost making, hessian sacking used over the top layer of compost will help to retain heat.

The 'Dalek'

For any one who hasn't seen the BBC TV programme Doctor Who, the 'Dalek' is an adopted name for the conical shaped compost bins that are cheap, readily available and probably the most common type of compost bin in Britain. Whilst they are not the natural choice for use with the Q.R. method, they are nevertheless very usable and can produce good compost. Since the Dalek was only really designed for cold composting, the drawback of using it with the Q.R. composting system (a 'hot' composting system)

The commonly used Dalek compost bin.

Worms devour the sacking material within the Dalek compost bin.

is that it quickly loses heat through its sidewalls, in particular in cold, wet, windy conditions. Therefore it is strongly advised that perennial weeds and any seeds do not enter the Dalek. If used in this manner with the Q.R. compost method then good compost making can still be achieved in the warmer seasons which is a vast improvement on the cold compost method for which they were intended. It is advisable to keep the Dalek as sheltered as possible to prevent windchill. A hessian sack stuffed with straw placed on top of the compost will greatly improve heat retention within the Dalek and once brandling worms enter or are added to your bin they will love to congregate within the hessian sack material when it's not to hot to do so. They will munch away at the sack material and can reduce it to tatters within a matter of weeks!

Miss Bruce adding garden waste to her railway sleeper compost bins.

CHAPTER 5

MATERIALS AND THEIR ADDITION TO THE
Q.R. COMPOST HEAP

The Q.R. compost heap, as far as I am aware, is a unique method of composting, the closest method to it being the biodynamic method with respect to the parallels between the herbs used in the Q.R. activator and the herbs used in the biodynamic preparations, but there I believe the similarities end. Quick Return composting has its own particular method of building the heap, as developed by Miss Bruce, and also has particular requirements about the type of materials used and the manner in which they are added to the heap. All this may sound very fussy and possibly awkward to achieve but it cannot be stressed enough how vitally important it is to ensure that the material going into the heap is of the correct type and size. Once this is understood it becomes second nature to follow and requires relatively little effort to execute. For clarity, this chapter is dedicated to the materials and how they should be prepared for addition to the Q.R. compost heap.

Because of the very different principles involved in the Q.R. composting process there are certain ideas that may work for methods such as 'cold' composting but do not work when using the Q.R. composting method. For example, adding scrunched up cardboard and newspaper and leaving lots of air gaps will actually hinder the Q.R. composting process, as will large lumps of any material. As far as Q.R. composting is concerned, small is best to ensure maximum surface area for microbes to work on and there are several ways that materials can be chopped or shredded in order to prepare them. The method of choice, and as advocated by Miss Bruce, is to chop material up using a spade but mechanised methods such as using a shredder or running over them with a lawn mower are also used, dependant upon the type of material. The end product of composting is in direct correlation with the quality of materials that are put into the heap, so if you put rubbish in, you will get rubbish out. The addition of fresh green materials full of vitality such as weeds or grass cuttings of a diverse nature (see later section on grass clippings) are essential to producing fertile compost. It is also a primary requirement to make the diversity of material as wide as possible, so this may mean collecting and storing certain materials such as nettle and comfrey leaves, ready to be added to the heap when required.

'Browns & Greens'

There are essentially two categories of material that can be added to the heap – these are materials with a high nitrogen (low carbon) content often known as 'greens' and materials with a high carbon (low nitrogen) content often known as 'browns'. Be careful though because some materials such as potato peelings are brown in colour but come under the 'green' category. As far as a ratio of browns to greens goes, I tend to aim for a 1:1 mixture by volume. This produces good temperatures as well as a good mix for ensuring that there are enough air pockets between the greens. 'Green' materials are generally softer in composition and break down relatively quickly; examples are grass

clippings, vegetable peelings and fruit. Their addition to the heap promotes bacterial action which produces a slightly more alkaline compost and therefore addition of large quantities of green material will result in a heap with a slightly higher ph value. This will be more likely to attract worms and less likely to attract slugs and snails.

'Brown' materials are generally more tough and woody and take longer to decompose. Wood contains cellulose and lignin which take a long time to break down and therefore wood chippings, twigs and sawdust should be kept to a minimum within the heap. They also require nitrogen to break down and can quickly use up the nitrogen available within the heap if allowed to do so. This 'robbing' of nitrogen can still be happening when the compost is added to the garden if the compost is not fully matured, particularly so if it is mixed in with the garden soil so care should be taken to ensure this doesn't happen. One way of using this type of compost is as mulch so that the minimum amount

Shredding woody herbaceous material.

of nitrogen is extracted from the soil. 'Brown' materials are broken down by the action of fungi and as a result produce a more acidic type compost. Examples of mainly carbon type materials are straw, hay, dried out stems of perennials, twigs and hedge clippings.

As with any material added to the heap, it is best to make them as small as possible to maximise the surface area available to the microbes in the compost and hence speed up their decomposition. I often run woody, dead perennial stems through the shredder to make a nice powdery friable mixture. Due to their woody nature, carbon type materials tend to be dry and should be thoroughly soaked for a minimum of 24 hours before adding to the heap. This can be done in a large container using rainwater, compost water or manure water. It also helps if you can add clay or clay type soil to the wetting mixture. This will serve two purposes; it will coat the material in tiny clay particles which will serve to absorb ammonia released as gas from the action of bacteria on nitrogen type materials such as grass clippings. It will also add fungi spores, as well as bacteria and other microbes which are essential to the composting process.

In my garden the quantity of greens is much greater than the quantity of browns produced which can be tolerated to a certain degree, however, sometimes sustainability is compromised and straw or other brown materials are imported to achieve a better mix. Since this is for the greater good of the heap and in turn the garden (and I can easily obtain straw from the local farm) I consider it to be acceptable.

The following table is a quick guide to summarise the brown and green categories:

BROWNS	GREENS
Hedge clippings	Grass clippings
Straw	Fresh weeds
Hay	Fruit
Herbaceous cuttings	Vegetable peelings
Softwood & hardwood cuttings	Comfrey
Bracken	Nettles
Autumn leaves	Manure

The individual characteristics and preparation methods for the main types of materials listed above are detailed as follows:

Grass Clippings Probably the most common material added to compost heaps. They should be preferably from lawns that are not treated with lawn care products such as moss killer and weed killer etc. The greater the diversity of flora and fauna in the clippings, the better since this will increase the diversity of life in the heap aiding in the production of the compost and increasing the nutrients it contains. I have encouraged as many forms of wild plants into my lawn as possible by not applying treatments and allowing wild flowers and herbs to seed themselves into it including yarrow, dandelion, daisy, plantain, clover, creeping buttercup and chamomile. I know this isn't many but in time others will arrive and on the occasions that I cut the grass it will please me to know that there is a greater diversity of animal life and plants going into the compost heap; including the herbs that make up the activator.

It is also advisable not to cut the lawn too short. Set the lawnmower cutting height to somewhere between 35mm and 50mm to enable flora and fauna to more readily exist in the lawn.

If possible, it is a good idea to mix the grass clippings with pre-wetted straw or woody material, to help break it up and prevent the loss of nitrogen as ammonia. If this happens, the smell will be very pungent and you will not be popular with your family or neighbours. The lawnmower can also be put to good use as a shredder and mixer of materials by strewing 'brown' material such as straw or hedge clippings over the lawn before it is cut. The lawn mower will pick these up chopping them and mixing them with the grass to give a well balanced and well mixed material.

Weeds The general consensus appears to be that plants that are in the wrong place are classified as a weed. From my point of view as a composter, a plant in the wrong place is a human opinion and not a plant's opinion; if anything, a plant that chooses to grow in a particular place usually finds its way there because the conditions are correct for its survival and hence 'weeds' are usually healthy plants that are anything but 'weedy' (perhaps 'weeds' should be renamed 'strays'?) The plants value to the compost heap is placed above all else. With this in mind 'weeding' takes on a different aspect and the value of the plants is appreciated and not wasted. The diversity and vitality of the plants that are added to the heap are crucial to its value as compost. Nowadays, I find fewer 'stray' plants in my borders due to the mulching with compost that usually happens about twice a year, however, as mentioned earlier, I try to allow as many different types of wild plant to exist in chosen areas of the garden such as the lawn, including those which are used in the activator. Unless they are added to the compost heap straight away, weeds should be stored in a covered container to retain their moisture and vitality until such time they can be added to the heap. It's important to add fresh weeds to your heap so that their vitality is given to the compost heap, contributing to the fertility of the compost and in turn to the plants that grow in the compost; this makes me feel less guilty when I'm pulling them up! In order to ensure that weed seeds and roots of perennial weeds are killed off, it is necessary for the heap to reach a temperature of 50° C for at least 3 days which is easily achieved if the Q.R. method is followed. When adding weeds to the heap it is best to place them in the middle of a layer where the heat will be greatest and they should be kept away from the top of an autumn heap where they may start to grow towards the light.

Comfrey If comfrey is available, it is a valuable addition to the Q.R. compost heap. It possesses about twice as much potash as good farmyard manure, is rich in protein but has little fibrous content (carbon) and therefore breaks down very quickly, even outside the compost heap. The best sort of comfrey for the garden (and the compost heap) is Bocking 14 which is richest in potassium and wilts quickly breaking down most rapidly. In his book, 'Comfrey, Past, Present and Future' Lawrence D. Hills stated in 1973 that comfrey is the fastest builder of vegetable protein yet known (the protein obtained from comfrey per acre can be nearly 20 times that taken from the soya bean) and is the only plant so far discovered to take vitamin B12 from the soil. Whilst this may be old information, they are still 'vital statistics'!

If you have the space available, a comfrey bed is a very useful asset and can provide material for the compost heap as well as being made into a nutritious liquid feed for hungry plants such as tomatoes. The feed is made by placing the comfrey leaves in a watertight container such as a water butt until it is about a quarter full then adding rainwater until it just covers the leaves. This should be left for a few weeks after which time the result should be a dark liquid with the leaves mainly disintegrated leaving a residue in the bottom of the can. The feed can be used by diluting it to a ratio of about 10 to 1. It is best to make it weaker rather than stronger since if too strong it can burn the plant's roots.

Nettles In particular, nettles are a very valuable commodity in providing an excellent accelerator especially if they are wetted and bruised when they will raise heat more quickly. They can still be available very late in the year; I have found them in sheltered parts of the garden in December and for a late autumn heap they can provide the kick start that it needs to get going.

If you have nettles in abundance they can also be used to make a liquid feed in the same manner as comfrey feed explained earlier. This results in quite a smelly concoction and its use as a feed is not quite as good as comfrey since it is lower in potassium.

Autumn Leaves Dead leaves from trees should not be added to the compost bin in large amounts since these are broken down by a different process. Small amounts mixed in with other materials won't make any difference, however, it they are added en masse, they will stick together and clog up the heap, halting the composting process. They are also poor in nutritional value and are best made into leaf mould in a separate bin of their own. They can be collected in black plastic bin bags, left over the winter and then treated with the Q.R. solution in the summer. This will produce a leaf mould that will be equivalent to that aged for a much longer period.

Kitchen Waste The waste that can be used from the kitchen in the compost bin is generally 'green' material and includes fruit and vegetable peelings, apple cores, banana skins, teabags, coffee grindings and residues, egg shells, and basically any vegetative material that hasn't been cooked. It is advisable not to put too much greasy/oily food in the compost since it will slow down the decomposition. Before it can be added to the heap, the kitchen waste must be chopped up with a spade and I have found that it is best to place the materials in a tough container which stops the materials from being spread around and also gives the spade something to chop against. A galvanised metal bucket is the best option but I have also used a very strong plastic box and a wooden box would also work. The chopping action of the spade quickly turns kitchen waste into a mushy consistency so it is best to mix them in the container with an equal amount of a coarser 'brown' material such as straw; this ensures that the right green to brown ratio is achieved. In addition, the water content of kitchen waste is usually very high, hence the mushy consistency, therefore mixing the waste with a dryish straw also helps to achieve the correct moisture levels.

Do not put any meat or fish into the compost bin, since these will attract flies and vermin. Although it is advisable not to attract mice to the heap, they will probably visit anyway because compost heaps are 'mouse paradise' in the cooler seasons due to the warmth and shelter provided and abundance of food and nesting material. Don't deter

Above:
Chopping up vegetative kitchen waste in a bucket.

Below:
A storage bin with cover to maintain the vitality of fresh green materials.

the mice unless they are a real problem. They will benefit the heap by reshuffling and mixing the materials as well as adding their waste to the heap.

Garden and Allotment Waste Towards the end of winter, the flower garden starts to look a bit shabby and the old dried out stems of the herbaceous borders require cutting back to allow the new growth to emerge and shown to full effect. This woody, old material is a welcome addition of carbon for the spring compost heap where it can be mixed in with the lush green cuttings from the lawn's first growth. The cuttings can be chopped on the ground with a spade and should be cut into pieces no longer than a few centimetres or, they can be shredded if desired. They should be soaked in rainwater or manure water for a couple of days otherwise they will be too dry to add to the heap. Waste from the allotment or vegetable garden such as wasted leaves from cauliflowers, lettuces, cabbage, parsnips, carrots, rhubarb etc., can be chopped with the spade and added to the heap. Even the tough stems from brassicas can be chopped up with the spade or bashed with the back of the spade to reduce them into small pieces. Pea and bean haulms as well as tomato stems can be treated similarly. Hedge clippings, detritus from under the hedge, soft wood and hardwood prunings, should either be shredded or run over with the lawnmower to chop them up.

Straw is an excellent addition to the heap and benefits the heap as a mixing material for soft green materials and as a source of air which is trapped in the tube like structures. Because it is usually very dry when it is acquired as a bale, it is advisable to soak it in a mixture of clay type soil and water for a few days, or better still, manure or compost water (see Chapter 8). This will ensure that the straw has a better chance of disintegration during the composting process.

Pet Litter Litter and bedding materials from pets such as rabbits, gerbils and hamsters are beneficial to the heap. Because this normally includes hay and straw which are relatively dry, it is best to soak them for a few days in manure or compost water. Bird droppings such as chicken manure are an excellent source of nitrogen and will provide tremendous heat when added to the heap. Avoid cat and dog litter at all costs.

Paper and Cardboard Despite their abundance and requirement for recycling, it is important that paper and cardboard are not added to the Q.R. compost heap because they will clog up and halt the Q.R. composting process. I have tried to use them shredded and in small amounts but even then they appear to remain unchanged and create anaerobic pockets within the heap. It is probably best that these materials are added to a worm bin.

Plastic and Metal Under no circumstances should these materials be added to the heap. Biodegradable plastics are used for some food packaging and should not be included since they will halt the Q.R. composting process in much the same way as paper and cardboard as described previously.

Urine Animal or human urine is an excellent activator, full of nitrogen, and can be included in the composting process. It is best not to add it straight into the heap since there is no way to ensure that it does not cool or saturate the heap. The best way to utilise its properties and control its application, is to wet dry brown materials with the urine before they are included in the heap. This is an ongoing process where urine is added (usually using a watering can!) to the contents of the storage bin where 'brown' materials are stored (see section on storing materials later in this chapter). If the urine is added in this way it will provide the following benefits: urine is nitrogen rich and will reduce the carbon to nitrogen ratio to a more acceptable level; it will increase the moisture in the dry brown materials to a level which is more suitable for composting; urine is an activator and it will help to start the decomposition process.

If you wish to add urine to the heap but you do not use a storage bin for your brown materials, then dry woody materials could be soaked in the urine before they are added to the heap which will provide the same benefits as previously stated.

Wood Ashes Wood ashes have high levels of potassium and can be included in the heap if desired, however, they are also alkaline in nature and therefore lime should not added to the heap if wood ashes have been added in sizeable quantities. Personally, I prefer to use wood ashes as a potash feed to fruit bushes and trees, by spreading it around the roots. It is best to do this annually, in the spring, at an application rate of no more than 450g per square meter.

Storing Materials for Composting

As materials become available for composting it is not always convenient to compost them straight away, particularly so if it is late autumn or winter or if you just simply wish to defer composting until a later date. In this case it is advisable to create some storage bins to accommodate the two different types of materials, namely 'browns' and 'greens'.

A storage bin for brown materials can be any large container that you can get your hands on. The only proviso is that it should have holes in the bottom to allow for

Wire containers are used for making leaf mould and storing 'brown' materials.

drainage. Materials such as straw, hardwood cuttings, hedge clippings, hay and herbaceous cuttings can be stored in this bin. If desired; urine (see earlier section in this chapter) manure water (see Chapter 8) or some soil water (rainwater with soil added; preferably clay type) can be applied to the materials with a watering can to coat them with these substances in readiness for composting.

Fresh 'green' materials such as weeds are best stored in a separate container which should be covered over with some weatherproof sheeting such as an old black plastic bin bag or something similar. The main purpose of this is to keep the material as fresh as possible by preventing it from drying out and losing its vitality. It is probably best to have drainage holes in the bottom of the container so that if any water does seep in then it can easily drain away.

The quick build wire netting bin makes an ideal storage container for materials waiting to be composted (see Chapter 4).

Adding the Materials to the Heap

When the materials have been prepared by chopping, shredding, wetting and soaking as appropriate they should be added to the heap in accordance with the Q.R. composting method for building the heap as detailed in the next Chapter.

CHAPTER 6

THE Q.R. COMPOSTING METHOD

The following method is almost identical to the original Q.R. method as detailed in Miss Bruce's books. It is suitable for most types of compost bin as detailed in Chapter 4. The method has been deliberately kept as simple as possible so that it can easily and quickly be referred to. The notes that follow the quick reference method expand on the individual steps, adding detail and reasoning to the procedures. It is beneficial and advisable to read and digest this Chapter and Chapter 3, 4 & 5 before attempting to go out there and start composting. The principal of making Q.R. compost is identical for whichever type of bin is used. The measurements and dimensions given are approximate.

Ten Step Quick Reference Method for the Q.R. Composting System

1. The compost bin should be sited on bare soil or grass if possible. If your soil is heavy clay and/or has poor drainage then place a 7cm layer of rubble/hard core/gravel in the bottom of the bin to provide drainage. Any aspect is okay except north facing.

   Preference would be for a sheltered, south facing aspect.

Step 1

Step 2

Step 3

Step 4

Step 5

Step 6

Step 7

2. Next, a ½" 2cm layer of crushed charcoal should be spread over the drainage material (if used). This absorbs any bad smells that the heap may produce. It's not absolutely necessary but Miss Bruce advised it.

3. Start building the layers of materials on top of the charcoal (see Chapter 5). Each layer should not be more than 10cm thick and it must be emphasised here that each layer is firmly packed. This is achieved by starting to pack the material from the outside edges and working towards the middle. Using a shovel or a rake can help with this when building layers at the bottom of the bin. Once you can reach inside the bin you can use your hands to position the material firmly in place.

4. Between each layer add a sprinkling of the Q.R. solution (see Chapter 7). When adding the solution it is important not to saturate the compost material. Placing your thumb over the end of the bottle to act as a sprinkler is okay ensuring that the surface of the heap is evenly covered. Approximately no more than 30ml should be added to each layer. Always add the solution immediately prior to the addition of a layer of material.

5. After adding each layer of material, it is desirable to incorporate some soil or mature compost. A small spadeful spread across the top of the layer is sufficient. If you are using lots of weeds in your heap then these will probably have enough soil on them so you shouldn't need to add anymore.

6. Layers should be varied or alternated if possible so that different types of material assist each other in allowing tiny spaces of air to exist. For example if a layer of grass cuttings is added (i.e. a soft mushy nitrogen type material), the next layer should preferably be a more coarse, carbon based type material such as straw. This also helps in getting the right carbon to nitrogen ratio which you should aim to be about 1 to 1 by volume but it's not critical. What's most important is that there are some quantities of each type of material.

7. After adding a couple of layers, the heap should be compacted down by light treading if possible. If you're athletic enough to get in the bin then do so. Your neighbours will think you are mad but they'll get used to it. If treading isn't an option then use the flat part of a rake. It's important to ensure that there is contact between the materials in the heap whilst at the same time ensuring that there is sufficient air. It is possible to over-compact the heap so be careful, however, once the composting process is under way, shrinkage of materials will ensure plentiful air passages.

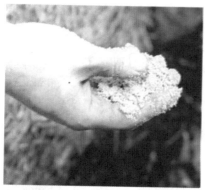

Step 8

Step 9

Step 10

8. After layering for approximately 30cm, it is advisable to add a dusting of crushed limestone. This assists in reducing the acidity of the heap, particularly if the heap is made from more nitrogen material than carbon material. Adding lime to the heap should be repeated at 30cm intervals. Lime should not be added to the heap if large quantities of manure are being used.

9. The heap is considered to be finished when the height of material is within 7cm of the top of the compost bin and no further material should be added. Whenever the addition of materials has been completed, cover the top of the heap with a hessian sack in order to keep heat within the bin (the temperature within the bin can easily reach 65 to 70°C). For ways of increasing and holding onto the heat, which are strongly recommended, see additional note later in this Chapter.

10. Next, place the lid or cover on the bin. This will prevent rain entering the bin since this would cool the compost and retard or even halt the composting process. When the compost is ready (after a minimum of four weeks), harvest the compost from the bin. This will be covered later in this Chapter.

Photograph of bin with slats removed. The finished compost is from the bin on the right. The bin on the left is a winter heap that has been recently reactivated and rebuilt with layers of fresh green material in the spring.

Building the Heap

The time taken to build the heap should not be longer than 4 weeks and layers of material should be added on a regular basis to ensure that the heat produced in the heap is maintained. Each time a new layer of material is added, the heating up process will be 'fuelled'. It is best to select a size of bin based on how much composting material you have available to ensure that the bin can be easily filled within 4 weeks. It is possible to sub-divide traditional bins with partitions to make smaller bins as appropriate (see Chapter 4). This may also be useful at the beginning of the composting season, in springtime, when there may be a shortage of ripe compost and you need to quickly build a heap to get a batch of compost as soon as possible. It can also be useful at the end of the season, in late autumn, when you want to get the process underway before it gets too cold. Remember that the time taken for 'the whole' heap to mature always commences from the date the heap was finished building. i.e. when the last piece of material was added. Material must not be added to the bin once it is full and it must be left to mature until ready.

Maturation of the compost can take place in as little as 4 weeks for a spring heap, 8 weeks minimum for a summer heap and 12 weeks minimum for an autumn heap. These are values quoted by Miss Bruce however my own efforts have usually been in excess of these periods by about 4 weeks. I expect the reasons for this are that I live about 300 miles further north than the Cotswolds where Miss Bruce lived and whilst my garden is at a similar altitude, it is quite exposed in comparison to Miss Bruce's sheltered walled garden. Good results are still achieved, but for less than optimum environmental conditions, I would add about 4 weeks on to the durations specified by Miss Bruce.

It is possible to build heaps in winter if materials are available, but decomposition is virtually brought to a standstill as is growth in the garden; the earth sleeps in winter taking the rest that it deserves, gathering reserves of nutrients and energy so that when spring arrives plants are ready to burst into life. The new lush spring growth is full of vitality. The winter heap can be reactivated by removing the top half of the heap and introducing a 4" (10cm) layer of fresh green material. Rebuild the rest of the heap in alternate layers of the winter material and the fresh greens. This heap will decompose very quickly, within 4 to 8 weeks and will be of excellent quality.

Treading the Heap

Large air gaps should be avoided since they will not allow the action of the Q.R. solution to permeate the heap (see Q.R. composting theory in Chapter 3). Contrarily, some air is required to let the heap breathe, it's a case of getting the balance right and this will come with experience. Light compaction of the heap is good, heavy treading and compaction is bad. It is advised that the heap should be compacted by light treading after the addition of a couple of layers to ensure that materials are virtually in contact with each other and any large air gaps created during subsidence are closed back up. Treading only applies to the building process and once the heap is built then it should be left to its own devices.

The Addition of Charcoal

In response to a letter to a composter, concerning the use of charcoal, Miss Bruce advised, "Charcoal has a unique cleansing property; it can absorb any poisonous gases that may be present and remain itself unchanged. That is why it is so used in filtering, as charcoal biscuits for indigestion and in many other ways, it just sweetens the heap."

The Addition of Lime

There are several different types of lime available, however, the type used in the compost heap should preferably be naturally occurring ground limestone. Since this is not a refined or chemically produced material it does not have any adverse affects on the life in the soil, however it should be used sparingly. F. H. Billington discusses the use of lime in his book 'Compost'. He advises that lime greatly stimulates and assists the activities of micro organisms in both soil and compost by breaking down resistant matter, reducing excess acidity and supplies the necessary base in the conversion of nitrogenous compounds into nitrates suitable for plant nutrition. Lime assists in improving the structure of soils by flocculating (adhering in flocks or flakes) the colloids (sticky substances) of clay which increases aeration and drainage. Lime will also increase the adhesion of sandy soils. There are obviously certain plants that are lime loving which include all legumes, turnips and beets and these will grow more readily in soils that have been inoculated with a compost that has been suitably limed. Lime can also be used to control diseases such as clubroot in brassicas.

Most limestone is mined, which strictly speaking is classed as an unsustainable source, however, if you are fortunate enough to live in a limestone area, you may possibly find chippings of limestone in your garden. To prepare them for use they can be crushed by pounding them with a hammer on a flat surface such as an old paving slab (don't forget your safety glasses and don't do it on the patio!). For most, probably the easiest and most sustainable way to obtain lime is as discarded egg shells from the kitchen. These can be readily turned into a powder by grinding them in a pestle and mortar. Other sustainable sources of lime include oyster shells and a product called Limex which is a co-product of the sugar beet industry, though I believe this may only be available on a commercial scale to farmers.

Increasing the Heat

It is very important to generate and retain as much heat as possible within the heap whilst also allowing the heap to breathe. Holding onto the heat for as long as possible will increase the speed of production. Miss Bruce's method of retaining and increasing the heat was to place weights on top of the hessian sacks. This was implemented either by placing large flat stones on top of the sacks, or heavy objects, such as stones or bricks on short boards on top of the sacks. I have tried this myself and it makes a considerable difference to the temperatures and speed of production. Another method which I use is to increase the amount of insulation on top of the heap. This can be achieved either by placing straw or any good insulating material within the hessian sacks or by adding a layer of thick insulation such as an old cushion from a chair or settee. If foam cushions are used they can absorb too much moisture from the heap therefore it is best to place them on top of a layer of plastic sheet.

The addition of wetted and bruised nettles to the heap will also generate a lot of heat, as will the addition of nitrogen rich chicken manure. Be careful how much chicken manure you add since large amounts can produce excess nitrogen in the compost leading to too much leafy growth in plants.

Harvesting the Compost

The compost is ready to use when it can no longer be discerned what it was originally made from. It will smell sweet and earthy and should be friable and easy to crumble. There may be some items which haven't broken down such as tough pieces of straw or wood. Sieve the compost to remove these and add them to the next compost heap.

When inspecting the compost for maturity, lift up the sacking and visually examine the contents beneath. If things look to be well decomposed then put your hands in or use a trowel to check the condition of the compost a few inches below the surface. If most things are disintegrated then it is ready. If you can still recognise most of the origins of the material then resettle the compost, replace the sack and covers and leave for at least a week before re-inspection.

Storing the Finished Compost

If the finished compost is to remain in the bin where it was made, a second bin will be required for building a new heap or alternatively the compost can be decanted and stored under cover or in a bag. Whilst the compost is covered it will continue to mature and improve. Miss Bruce advised that it can be stacked into a steeply sided heap and then covered with soil so that rain runs off. I cannot comment on how long it can be stored for since it nearly always gets put to use within a couple of months.

The Method for the Farm Heap

Miss Bruce developed the Q.R. compost method for farms and whilst I have no experience of its application to the farm, I feel that it could be of particular benefit to farmers to include it. In particular, there are sometimes large amounts of straw that appear to be left to rot in the fields these days when they could be turned into valuable compost. The following method is quoted from her book 'Common Sense Compost Making':

"It is obviously impossible to have bins all over the farm; therefore, farm heaps must be built in the open, and, as farm material is brought in by the cart-load, instead of the barrowful, they must be of larger dimensions. A section eight feet long by six feet wide and six feet high is a useful size. One section can be completed before going on to the next; the sections can touch, and so make an ever lengthening clamp. If the top is sharply ridged rain will not seep in. The procedure of building is the same as for the garden heap. Good drainage is necessary. Build in layers of four inches. If there is a mass of one material, break it by narrow layers of soil, or better still manure. This should be available on the farm and can be used in two-inch layers throughout the heap. Material like old dry hay, tough grass, and above all, dry straw, should be saturated with treated manure water (see Chapter 8 – A.E.D.)....If a farm is equipped with a urine tank, the tank itself can be treated. Soak some sand, or dry soil, in the diluted Q.R. solution, allowing one pint to each cubic foot of tank space. Scatter the soaked sand over the surface. The sand will sink, and free the solution to do its work from the bottom. Straw soaked, or even sprayed with this urine, would make valuable compost, and break down very quickly.

In an all straw heap, include if possible two-inch layers of fresh green nettles or bracken. The green gives vitality; nettles wetted and bruised will raise heat more quickly than anything! Manure, if possible, otherwise soil in narrow layers, will steady the heap. Treat it; it will go to rich black mould, without turning, in from four to six months. It can then be spread with a shovel."

Failures and Their Remedies

On the rare occasions that failure occurs, it is usually because there is a breakdown of one or more of the four primary conditions for Q.R. composting, as detailed in Chapter 3, and as follows:

1. Loss of Shelter
2. Loss of Heat
3. Lack of Aeration
4. Poor Drainage

The table overleaf is provided, with causes and remedies as advocated by Miss Bruce, to help diagnose and rectify problems that may arise;

Symptom	Cause	Remedy
Heap Dried Out.	Sacking omitted from top layer of compost causing loss of heat and moisture retention.	Pour over one gallon (4.5l) of manure or compost water and replace sacking and shelter.
Rain drenched Heap.	Shelter not provided.	Fork the compost into piles and let sun and air get to it for a few days. Wet with manure water and leave for a few weeks.
Putrefaction and bad smells.	Lack of aeration due to inadequate ventilation.	Ensure that adequate spaces are provided in the walls of the bin. Fork the compost into piles and let sun and air get to it for a few days. Wet with manure water and leave for a few weeks.
	Lack of aeration due to over compaction, possibly due to heavy treading.	Fork the compost into piles and let sun and air get to it for a few days. Wet with manure water and leave for a few weeks.
	Lack of aeration in base due to poor drainage.	Ensure that adequate drainage is provided by the addition of rubble in the base of the enclosure. Fork the compost into piles and let sun and air get to it for a few days. Wet with manure water and leave for a few weeks.
Heap not disintegrated on opening of the heap after prescribed period.	Heap opened too early.	Leave for at least a week then re-examine.
Heap not disintegrated after much longer than specified period.	Q.R. activator omitted or use of old Q.R. activator.	Remake the heap with fresh green layers and treat with fresh Q.R. activator.

Q.R. sales leaflet. *(Courtesy of Chase Organics)*

CHAPTER 7

THE ACTIVATOR, THE HERBS & THE HONEY

The herbs used in the Q.R. compost activator are no secret and are those that Rudolph Steiner used for the biodynamic preparations as advocated in his 1924 lectures and are namely; valerian, nettle, yarrow, dandelion, chamomile and oak bark. Miss Bruce took the herbs and made her own preparations which were entirely different to those made by the Anthroposophical Agricultural Foundation[1]. ('it was not Dr. Steiner who had given either dandelions or nettles to the world' as she advised the association). As explained in Chapter 1, Miss Bruce originally made the activator in the form of a solution and later as a powder. The formula for the power is provided since the method of preparation is easier and better results are achieved.

Cautionary Note

Whilst some varieties of plants are protected under the Wildlife and Countryside Act 1981, it appears that the herbs used in the Q.R. activator are not protected species and most are relatively common. The countryside agency advise on their website(cms.ed.countryside access.gov.uk) that picking of small amounts of common flowers for one's own use may be deemed acceptable by custom but this may deprive other people of the privilege of seeing them. Wild flowers should not be picked unless there are in abundance with plenty left for the enjoyment of others nor should any plant be uprooted.

As an alternative to picking the flowers from the wild, it is suggested that you could do one of the following:

> *1. Grow the herbs yourself from seed purchased from a reputable supplier*
>
> *2. Purchase the herbs from a reputable supplier*
>
> *3. Purchase the Q.R. powder from Chase Organics Ltd.(see chapter 9 for contact details)*

(1) The English branch of Dr. Steiners's Biodynamic Association.

Formula for the Q.R. Powder

The formula for making the powder is given as follows and is in principle, that which is detailed in Miss Bruce's book 'Common Sense Compost Making':-

Ingredients;

1. Chamomile *(Matricaria Chamomilla)*
2. Dandelion *(Leontodon Taraxacum)*
3. Valerian *(Valeriana Officinalis)*
4. Yarrow *(Achillea Millifolium)*
5. Nettle *(Urtica Dioica)*
6. Powdered Oak bark
7. Pure Run Honey

Method; Flowers and leaves are gathered before midday. They should be dried out as soon as possible with slow heat, i.e. on a radiator. When tinder dry, crush with a pestle and mortar or you could use a mechanical grinder. Pass the herbs through a fine wire kitchen sieve keeping each of the herbs separate.

The oak bark is prepared by filing it with a rough file or rasp to make a fine powder and then passing it through a fine sieve.

The honey is prepared by rubbing one drop of honey into a teaspoonful of powdered baby milk or dried milk.

Stock Mixture; Take a level teaspoon of each ingredient, mix them thoroughly and keep in an air tight jar.

The powder can be made into a solution as detailed in the next section and added to the heap as detailed in Chapter 6.

Making Up a Dosage Bottle of Q.R. Solution from the Powder

The solution should be made by the addition of one pint of rainwater (bottled spring water is okay) to **ONE PINCH** (or a flat teaspoon) of the Q.R. powder in a bottle with a screw top; old wine or beer bottles are ideal for this purpose. Do not be tempted to add more than the stated amount of powder since the principle is essentially homeopathic. The mixture should be shaken up and left to stand for 24 hours before addition to the heap. The solution has a sweet smell and should be kept in a cool dark place, preferably somewhere near to the compost bin for ease of use.

It can be kept for up to approximately one month. If it smells sour then make up a fresh batch of solution. The powder can be kept indefinitely if stored in the right conditions, but it is good idea to buy a new batch annually in the spring. This avoids building heaps with powder that may be off and thereby a waste of time and effort.

The Herbs

The herbs used in the activator have special individual healing powers, nutritional value, mineral content, medicinal properties, spiritual significance and everyday uses. It is almost uncanny that the herbs used in the activator are amongst those that have been most widely used throughout history for their ability to heal, soothe, protect and charm and have become sacred and embroiled into our existence; deeply associated with mystery, folklore, superstition, religion and magic.

Many assets, properties and uses of the herbs are given so that if they are grown in the garden, advantage can be taken of these. Propagation advice is also given, should you wish to grow the herbs, and details of their habitats are listed, should you wish to pick the herbs.

Plants can often vary in the amounts of minerals they contain which can be dependant on location and weather conditions; flower solutions made from locally grown herbs will be in harmony with the soil, giving it the nutrients it lacks when the compost is worked into the soil. Miss Bruce observed that between them they contain all the essential mineral elements to plant life. This could also be said for a different group of herbs, however, Miss Bruce always included nettle and honey in her formula since these are both powerful compost activators and without these results were impaired. Besides these two components, Miss Bruce tried replacements of coltsfoot and plantain. There are many possibilities for making the formula from different herbs and experimentation in this area should be encouraged.

Cautionary Note

The following information is not provided as a means of diagnosing ailments and prescribing suitable herbs. It is purely for information purposes only. For the diagnosis and treatment of ailments using herbs, a suitably qualified herbal practitioner should be consulted.

Chamomile
(Matricaria Chamomila)

History and Custom Chamomile is a member of the aster family and is a native of Europe. It is also known as whig plant, ground apple or earth apple. When the plant is crushed a pleasant apple like fragrance is emitted and hence its Latin name is derived from *kamai* meaning 'on the ground' and *melon* meaning apple. It was regarded as one of the sacred herbs of Woden. To the Anglo-Saxons it was known as 'Maythen' and was chosen as one of their Nine Herbs Lay in the Lacnunga, an early Anglo-Saxon manuscript. In ancient Egypt the plant was a sacred healing herb, dedicated to their sun god and was used by the priests who devoted their lives to healing the sick in the House of Life; the sacred building situated next to most of the temples. The Egyptians used the herb to treat many ailments including colds, fever, aches and pains and so called female disorders. It was believed by the ancient Romans that it was an antidote to serpent bites and in the late 19th century it was used as a substitute for quinine in the treatment of malaria. People with consumption (tuberculosis) were advised by doctors to sit next to chamomile beds to breathe in the scent of the herb. When chamomile was first introduced into North America it was used as a poultice on wounds to prevent gangrene.

Chamomile was a sacred healing herb to the ancient Egyptians.

Appearance and Habit This is the annual true chamomile or 'German' chamomile and should not be confused with the perennial 'Roman' chamomile (Anthemis Nobilis) used for making lawns. It is distinguished from other similar looking daisy type flowers by its conical yellow receptacle which is hollow in the case of true chamomile but not so in other similar flowers. It can grow to 15 in. (40cm) high and has 15 white ray type florets around the receptacle. During flowering the receptacle bends upwards into a cone, giving rise to the characteristic hollowness. The cone is covered with a mass of yellow tubiform florets which all open fully when the dome is at its highest. Masses of seeds are produced which can germinate very quickly and plants can flower within eight weeks of sowing.

The leaves are bright green, delicate and fern like and at their most lush when the plant is not flowering. The plant appears to put most of its energies into flowering which is over a long period, between June and September.

The plant is often found growing at the roadside, in rough fields and at the edges of wheat fields when not restricted by the application of herbicides.

Propagation The plant is an annual and has to be grown from seed, however, it self seeds freely so once established it will appear in various places around the garden. It can either be sown in early spring or autumn in rows 8 to 12 in. (20 to 30cm) apart. The seeds are very fine and therefore should be sown on a still, preferably humid day and mixed with sand or wood ashes. Whilst the germination progress is going on it is advisable to keep the seedbed moist.

Nutrients The plant contains potash, lime, phosphorous and sulphur.

Reputed Medicinal Properties The true chamomile is the one used more for medicinal purposes and has a healing blue oil which is part of a chemical substance called Azulene. This has an anti inflammatory effect. On wet or foggy days there may be only half the amount of essential oil and therefore the herb should only be harvested when it is dry and sunny.

The flowers of the true chamomile contain volatile oils, resins, bitter substances, wax, fats and glycoside which have an antispasmodic effect. They have a pleasant flavour and a cleansing, soothing action on the stomach and mucus lined organs.

When made in to a tea, it has a calming effect and is an aid to digestion after heavy meals. A tea made from chamomile flowers and peppermint leaves can settle an upset stomach. Due to the anti bacterial and anti inflammatory qualities of the herb, an infusion, combined with sage, used as a gargle, can give relief from sore throats and inflamed gums.

Chamomile makes an excellent facial steam bath either for a heavy cold or for improving the condition of the skin. It is useful as a hair rinse and as an eye bath in the case of inflammation of the eye lids. It can also be used as a mouthwash and has anti pain properties making it useful after dental treatment, for compresses, toothache and a sore mouth. An infusion, made from two teaspoons of flowers per cup of boiling water allowed to brew for five to ten minutes, can be applied as a warm rinse. Alternatively a small linen bag filled with the flowers can be warmed on a kettle or hot water bottle to hold against the part that requires pain relief.

Chamomile can also be used against eczema or skin problems relating to old age.

Precautions The plant has no known side effects.

Other Properties and Uses Chamomile has a restoring or healing virtue to ailing or sick plants when planted beside them. It is sometimes known as the "the plant doctor", and is said to increase the production of essential oils in plants growing beside it. The fresh flowers can be added to bathwater to aid relaxation. In Spain, it is apparently added as a flavouring to sherry.

Dandelion
(*Leontodon Taraxacum*)

Dandelions proliferating in a wild flower meadow.

History and Custom This most common of herbs, considered by many as a weed, is a very nutritious and useful plant. It was first recognised in Europe in the 10th and 11th centuries but was known much earlier in Chinese medicine. It has many other names including devil's milkwort, clockflower, horselettuce, dog's posy and swines snout. Many of its names, such as jack-piss-the-bed, mess-a-bed, pee-a-bed, pissy bed, pis-en-lit are as a result of its strong diuretic properties. In Ireland it is known as heart-fever-grass due to its reputation as 'a sovereign remedy against swooning and passions of the heart'. The name dandelion is possibly of Norman origin and comes from the jagged edges of the leaves; hence 'dent de lion' or 'lion's tooth'. Culpepper held the herb in high esteem; 'You see here what virtues this common herb hath, and that is the reason the French and the

Dutch so often eat them in the spring; and now if you look a little farther, you may see plainly without a pair of spectacles, that foreign physicians are not so selfish as ours are, but more communicative of the virtues of plants to people'. In Victorian Britain, dandelion stout was common and sold for 2d a bottle.

Appearance and Habit There is not much need here to describe the dandelion's appearance since it is recognised by virtually everyone and will grow almost anywhere, even in almost completely shaded conditions. Despite it being very common and disregarded by so many, it is a very special herb with a deeply penetrating root system that is formed before the plant is able to produce its true flowers. This root system is quite slow to develop, taking almost a year with the gradual building up and orientation of the leaves through the plants first summer. If a plant is germinated from seed in the spring, it will flower the following spring, however if a plant is germinated from seed in the autumn, it will not flower until the spring of its second year. The plant flowers from April to October and there is a dramatic flush of dandelions in May, which can be quite a spectacle at the roadsides on our country lanes and a welcome sign of summer looming.

Propagation The plant is a perennial and self seeds freely as well as having the promiscuity of a root system of which even a small part will take readily producing a new plant and it is for these reasons that the plant has become so maligned. The fruit of the plant can also develop without cross-fertilisation. Seed should be sown in April.

 Nutrients The plant contains high levels of potassium, iron, phosphorous, calcium, manganese, sodium, silicic acid and cholin which can also be found in the gall bladder. The roots contain inulin.

Reputed Medicinal Properties During winter, green dried leaves can be taken to improve the function of the gall bladder and it has also been said that it can eradicate gall and kidney stones. It stimulates digestive glands and increases the action of the gall bladder and pancreas. The whole of the plant has uses for liver problems and can be used to treat jaundice. An infusion made from the dried root stimulates the production of bile. In Chinese medicine it is used to treat mastitis, breast cancer, tumours, abscesses, hepatitis and jaundice. The milky juice in its leaves and stems have been used to remove pimples and warts.

Precautions The plant has diuretic properties so should be taken in moderation.

Other Properties and Uses A coffee like drink can be made from the ground dried root of dandelion. The roots should be dried until they are brittle. The young leaves are a useful addition to a springtime salad, reported to be higher in nutritional value than spinach and is also a good cleanser of the blood. The flowers can also be eaten and are said to be quite sweet. The leaves are excellent when chopped and cooked in butter with lemon or cider-vinegar.

Valerian
(Valeriana Officinalis)

History and Custom This native of Europe and Western Asia is also known as phu, garden heliotrope, all-heal and setwall. It is an old highly valued Nordic medicinal plant and it was used extensively as a medicine in the 5th and 4th centuries B.C. at the time of Hippocrates. It was also used in Anglo Saxon recipes of the eleventh century. The name comes from the Latin *valere* meaning to be healthy. Apparently cats and rats have a strange fascination for it; cats will roll in it and will go into a kind of trance in the same way they do when they come across catmint (nepeta), rats will dig up the roots and behave in a similar fashion. It is said that the pied piper of Hamelyn carried valerian roots on his body. Earthworms also have an attraction for the plant. The plant is dedicated to St Bernard and

Valerian has a calming effect on the whole nervous system.

has associations with inspiring love; it was believed that if a girl wore valerian, she would never be without a lover. It was also said to protect people from thunder and lightning and had uses for and against witchcraft. The plant was cultivated by the 'valerie growers' of Derbyshire and sold to the drug companies for its sedative properties.

Appearance and Habit Valerian is a hardy perennial, growing from 3 to 5ft high. The stems terminate in 2 or more pairs of flowering stems and have deep grooves running down them which are mainly covered in hairs. The leaves are dark green, irregularly divided, pinnate and covered with short soft hairs underneath. Dense clusters of small tubular, pink or white flowers appear between June and September, followed by tiny seeds with a tuft of white hair. The flowers have a distinctive smell, something like vanilla, which can be quite overpowering giving rise to its old country name of phu. The root is a short thick rhizome from which many fine, tentacle like roots grow out like a head of hair. Runners are thrown out from the base of the stems.

It can be found in damp areas such as ditches, near streams and at roadsides and verges in the UK. Most types of soil will accommodate valerian and although it prefers moist conditions it will also tolerate exposed positions.

Propagation The plant is a perennial and can be propagated either by division of root or from seed, however, propagation from seed is relatively poor having only about a 50% success rate. The seeds germinate very slowly so they should either be sown in rows or sown with a marker crop. The seeds germinate in the light and do not need covering; a light pressing onto the surface of the soil will suffice. If planting for a crop then plants should be spaced 12" (30cm) apart and rows should be 2 to 3ft (60 to 90cm) apart. During the first year the plants will probably not flower, if they do, they should be cut off while the plants are developing to promote rhizome development.

Nutrients The plant contains potash, lime, phosphorous and sulphur.

Reputed Medicinal Properties Valerian has a calmative effect due to the presence of valepotriates. It also contains volatile oil and a glycoside. It promotes sleep and is used in many of the commercial type sleep remedies. It is mainly used to treat nervous tension, anxiety, headaches, indigestion, insomnia and for lowering blood pressure. Valerian also possesses antispasmodic properties and is used to treat stomach cramps, irritable bowel syndrome, nervous dyspepsia and menstrual cramps. The roots of the plants are used and should be dried in the dark before use. Valerian tea is one of the strongest sedatives that can be made from a plant; it has a calming effect on the whole nervous system and is an excellent tranquilizer. It has been discovered that the bacteria that cause typhoid are destroyed within 45 minutes when subjected to air impregnated with the vapours of valerian oil.

Precautions It is not advisable to take large doses and continuous use should be avoided. A few days break should be taken after using for a couple of weeks.

Other Properties and Uses Tincture of valerian is said to cure dandruff. It is also reputed to have been used as a spice and as a perfume in the sixteenth century and was laid amongst clothes. Probably due to its pungent smell, the plant has been used in many countries to ward off evil spirits over the centuries.

According to Gertrud Frank in her book 'Companion Planting', a fermented liquid, made from the plant in the same manner as comfrey or nettle liquid, can be applied to all flowering and fruiting plants including beans, peas, tomatoes, cucumbers and courgettes. It is best applied early in the year and should not be applied to onion and carrots or lettuce. The mixture is mild but very effective and is particularly noteworthy when applied to irises and roses which apparently bloom as never before.

Miss Bruce's advice to help cuttings take more readily and make good roots was to soak them in valerian juice (10,000 to 1 ratio) for 24 hours.

Yarrow
(Achillea Millifolium)

History and Custom This herb is a native of Western Asia and Europe and is also known as soldier's woundwort, knyten milfoil, sanguinary, nosebleed and thousand leaf. Yarrow leaf is used by the Chinese in traditional herbal medicine. Yarrow stems are used in an ancient ceremony of divination (telling the future) in the 'Yarrow Stalk Oracle' also known as the 'I Ching' or book of changes. The Latin name *achillea* is derived from the Greek hero Achilles, allegedly the first person to use the herb to heal wounds. Apparently Achilles treated the wounds of his soldiers at the battle of Troy and it has since been used many times on the battlefield throughout history. The French know the herb as 'herbe au charpentier', being renowned for its ability to heal the wounds inflicted by the use (or misuse) of carpenters tools. The Anglo-Saxons named the herb 'gearwe' which means 'repairer of bodies'. In 19th century Ireland the herb was considered a lucky charm because of the belief that yarrow was the first

Yarrow was sacred to the ancient druids who used the stalks to predict the weather.

herb picked by Jesus as a child. The herb was sacred to the druids who used the stalks to predict the weather. It is believed that yarrow had powers for and against witchcraft; it was used by witches in potions and spells, some names for the herb link it with the devil such as devil's plaything, devil's condiment and devil's nettle. It was also used to protect against evil spirits and was hung in houses on St John's eve (23rd June). Woven garlands of the herb were used for decoration and were said to ward off fairies and witches. There are many superstitions associated with the herb; it was believed that carrying yarrow in a wedding bouquet known as 'seven years love' would ensure that the love between the bride and the groom would last for at least seven years. Another said that if a woman picked the herb from the grave of a young man on the night of a full moon and placed it under her pillow, she would dream of her future lover. As a healing herb, there are few herbs as well respected, and it became known as the iodine of the meadows and fields. The herb developed a reputation for relief of fevers giving rise to the name 'fever herb'. Traditionally the herb was used to treat rheumatism.

Appearance and Habit Yarrow is a hardy perennial and grows from 1 to 3ft high in sun or light shade. The white and pink flowers, which appear from June to September, are strongly but not unpleasantly scented. The leaves are usually dark green, narrow, aromatic, lacy and finely divided which give rise to its name milfoil or thousand leaves.

Yarrow is very common and can be found on hillsides, dry pastures and by the roadside.

Propagation The plant is a perennial which self seeds freely and has creeping roots so it can be quite rampant if allowed to do so. It can be propagated by division of the roots or from seed which can be sown from spring through to autumn.

Nutrients The plant contains iron, lime, nitrates, potash, phosphorous, soda and sulphur.

Reputed Medicinal Properties Contains tannins which help to heal wounds and flavonoids which dilate peripheral arteries encouraging better blood flow to the skin. This cools any fever, lowers blood pressure and also eliminates blood clots. Used to treat rheumatism, colds and flu, external and internal bleeding, and haemorrhoids and stimulates the digestive system. For a herbal tea, use 1 teaspoon of fresh or dried herb to 1 cup of boiling water, the taste is not unpleasant and is peppery but slightly bitter.

Precautions If the leaves are too frequently used on the skin, it can become sensitive to light and sunburn.

Other Properties and Uses The infused leaves make a good skin freshener and toner and were once used as flavouring for beer.

Nettle
(Urtica dioica)

History and Custom This European native originated in the Mediterranean regions. The latin name *urtica* originates from Pliny, and comes from urere which means to burn, as a result of its stinging hairs. Traditionally the Romans are said to have introduced a rarer form of the herb to Britain; *U. pilulifera,* known as the roman nettle and it is believed they used to whip themselves with nettles to help them endure the bitterly cold British winters.

Nettles stimulate the circulation and lower the blood pressure.

Appearance and Habit The plant is an unbranched, tough, spreading perennial, about 2 to 4ft high (60 to 120cm), and often forms large clumps due its creeping root system. The heart shaped leaves are toothed, the flowers are catkin like and are usually green but can sometimes have a purple tint. Male and female flowers appear on separate plants and flowering takes place between July and September. The stem and the leaves are covered in stinging hairs.

Nettles will grow wild on virtually any soil but prefer fertile (nitrogen rich) soil and are often seen growing in areas where there are, or have been, human settlements. They are also usually found on waste land, in gardens, road sides, field edges etc.

Propagation The plant is a promiscuous self-seeder and can also spread via its creeping rootstock.

Nutrients   It is claimed that the plant contains iron, magnesium, silicic acid, formic acid, sodium, potassium, calcium and vitamins A, B and C.

Reputed Medicinal Properties   The young leaves of nettles have special curative properties in that they are haematinic and increase the haemoglobin in the bloodstream. The poison created by nettles is a substance similar to histamine and the hormone created by the pancreas. The plant has many healthy giving properties and with the benefit of its mild pleasant taste, it is a herb that we should possibly make regular use of. The plant has diuretic properties. It is also used to treat gout and arthritis and is thought to stimulate the excretion of uric acid. Nettles have been used to reduce bleeding, ease excessive menstruation, lower blood sugar, and encourage the flow of breast milk. The plant became an established method for curing rheumatism by whipping the body with them. The plant stimulates the circulation and lowers blood pressure. Haemorrhoids can be treated by taking nettle tea.

Precautions   Older plants can be toxic eaten raw and may cause kidney damage therefore only young plants should be used.

Other Properties and Uses   There is an organic salt within nettles that is not a burden on the kidneys and therefore the plant can be used by people in a salt reduced diet. The young leaves can be made into a herbal tea or soup and also used as a vegetable (the sting disappears when the leaves are boiled or dried). Nettles are used in hair treatments and shampoos, for preventing baldness, the treatment of dry scalp, reducing dandruff and making the hair glossy. They are grown commercially for their high chlorophyll content which is used to colour foods and medicines. As an excellent companion plant; it helps neighbouring plants to be more resistant to disease; it increases the content of essential oils in neighbouring herbs and stimulates the formation of humus. Nettle stems can be woven into a cloth and also make a strong twine or rope. During the First World War, nettle fibre was used to make army clothing. It has also been used for making sailcloth, sacking, sheets, cloth and muslin (hence the German name for muslin is Nessel-tuch or nettle cloth). When wetted, bruised and added to the compost heap, they make an excellent activator, producing high temperatures (they can be used alongside the Q.R. activator without causing problems). And last but not least, nettles have been used to make beer!

Oak Bark
(*Obtained from English or Pedunculate Oak Quercus robur*)

History and Custom This tree is considered by most as a very English tree and by long tradition is the national tree of England. It has strong affinity with shipbuilding and England's 'wooden walls', and the qualities of the oak have even been linked to the strength of the nation. A shanty written by David Garrick in the mid 18th century captures the relationship between the oak and Englishmen in the two lines 'Heart of oak are our ships, Heart of oak are our men'. The common oak tree is infamous with tradition, magic and mystery probably more so than any other plant or herb. It was said to be used in the ceremonies of the ancient druids and believed to protect buildings and their inhabitants from lightning strikes, particularly so if the tree was planted adjacent to buildings and hence lightning would be attracted to the tree rather than the building. It was once believed that if an acorn was carried it would preserve youth. Oak trees can live for over 500 years and become local landmarks, pubs are named after them, children

Oak was used in the ceremonies of the ancient druids.

play in or near them, they become monumental and symbolic, they acquire there own names such as the 'Milking Oak' in Salcey Forest Northamptonshire, where the cows that grazed under it were milked there in rainy or very hot weather (from the book 'Flora Britannica' by Richard Mabey). There are also famous oak trees such as the Major- Oak in Sherwood forest which is popularly thought to be the hiding place of Robin Hood and his Merry men. The largest oak tree recorded is the Newland Oak with a girth of 45ft. The pagan symbol, the green man, has oak leaves emerging from his mouth and ears, and this symbol can be seen carved in some of our old churches.

Appearance and Habit The oak is a deciduous, monoecious tree which can grow as high as 25m (82ft). It has wide spreading branches and rugged grey-brown bark. The leaves are small dark green and ovate with deeply rounded lobes. Both sexes of flower appear on the same tree in May; the male flower is a slender pale green catkin, the female flowers are less conspicuous and are borne in spikes in the leaf axils followed by ovoid fruit in little cups (acorns) on the end of the stalks. The acorn and cup are green to begin with becoming brown by autumn. The bark is smooth and greyish-brown in young trees, but later becomes more rugged and fissured. Beneath the bark the sapwood is white, while the heartwood is a rich golden brown colour. If you are collecting oak bark from the wild, it should be taken from dead trees that have been felled or damaged due to the elements. It is not always easy to identify from the bark alone, so it is best to take bark from fallen branches that can easily be recognised by leaves that are present on the tree in summer or in the ground in autumn/winter.

The tree is native to Europe and is often found on clay type soils. It can be found in forests, woodland, parkland and open fields when allowed to do so.

It is believed that the tree is host to approximately 350 species of insects. After its death, an oak tree continues to support life with more than 200 varieties of fungi living on the decaying wood as well as many insects.

Propagation   Acorns can be planted in containers in the autumn but are very slow growing.

Nutrients   Oak bark contains potassium, lime and calcium.

Reputed Medicinal Properties   Oak bark is believed to control bleeding and also has anti inflammatory and antiseptic qualities. The bark can be applied externally to treat cuts, abrasions, ulcers, skin irritations, varicose veins, and haemorrhoids. It is sometimes taken internally to treat haemorrhaging, diarrhoea, and upset stomachs.

Other Properties and Uses   The wood of oak is extremely durable and was used in shipbuilding, furniture making and structural members in buildings. Acorns are mixed with beech nuts to provide pannage for pigs (pannage is the practise of turning out domestic pigs into woodland or forest to forage on the bounty of natural food crops such as beech mast and acorns). Oak bark yielded tannin for leather and branches were turned into charcoal for smelting iron.

Honey

History Honey has been used for its medicinal qualities for over 4000 years. The Egyptians had over 500 medical formulae based on honey. The Greeks used it to cure skin disorders. It is an ancient remedy for healing infected wounds; in c. 50AD Dioscorides described honey as a good treatment for rotten and hollow ulcers. In the early part of the 20th century it was demonstrated that the anti bacterial effects of honey are increased when it is diluted due to the presence of an enzyme within the honey.

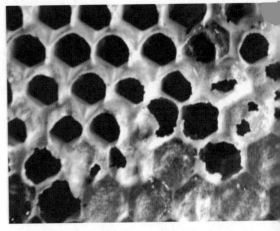

Nutrients Honey contains fructose, glucose, enzymes, sugars, gluconic acid, vitamins, minerals and amino acids.

Reputed Medicinal Properties It has been reported by scientists that honey has an anti inflammatory effect and promotes the growth of healing

Honey is an ancient remedy for healing infected wounds.

tissues, speeding up the healing process. In the developed world antibiotics have taken over from honey as an antibacterial agent, however, with the increased tolerance of bacteria to these drugs, interest in honey has recently been reawakened as a method of fighting against infections.

Dr Peter Charles Molan, from the Honey Research Unit in Waikato, New Zealand, published a report in 2001, stating that in lab studies it has been shown that honey has an antimicrobial action against a wide range of bacteria and fungi. The antibacterial effects of honey are due to the release of low levels of hydrogen peroxide, by the enzyme glucose oxidase, when honey is diluted. Manuka honey from New Zealand has a phytochemical component and is particularly useful in treating wound pathogens where orthodox medical treatments have failed.

Honey is hygroscopic in its nature and will therefore draw in moisture from the surrounding air. When honey is applied to wounds; they heal more quickly, scars are prevented, the growth of new tissue is assisted and bandages will not adhere to an open wound.

Precautions Honey should not be given to infants under 12 months old as this may lead to poisoning. Honey should be eaten in moderation due to its high sugar content.

Other Properties and Uses Honey does not deteriorate; jars of honey were discovered in the tomb of King Tutankhamen which were apparently still edible after more than 3,000 years. The hygroscopic property of honey has made it useful in the cosmetics industry for preventing skin drying out, keeping it moist and fresh. Honey contains many antioxidants important in the elimination of free radicals.

In my personal experience, in writing this book, I was reading about the healing effects of honey and in particular how it was effective against most common skin fungi called dermatophytes. At the time I was suffering from an irritating fungal infection which had been persisting for some time despite the application of prescribed creams from my doctor. I abandoned the creams and applied the honey twice a day, diluted in a ratio of 7 to 1. Within 2 weeks the infection disappeared completely and has not returned since.

Success has prevailed in the flower, fruit and vegetable gardens where previously most of my gardening efforts ended up in failure.

CHAPTER 8

USING THE COMPOST AND THE RESULTS

It's a very exciting day when, after the weeks of waiting in anticipation, the covers on the heap are drawn back to reveal rich fertile compost. The ripe compost will be a dark sweet smelling friable mixture of small fibrous type objects and you won't be able to work out what the majority of it was made from. There will probably be a few tough stems or twigs which have been too tough to breakdown, and straw is also sometimes difficult for the heap to deal with completely. When you run the compost through your fingers it will feel cool and soothing and for that sensation alone it is worth the hard effort put in!

The true rewards come when the compost is applied to the soil. You will not just be adding food to the soil, you are adding life! Life will inoculate the soil, spreading through it, adding its fertility, dispersing the humus through out the soil. Life and death will go on in the soil with the release of nutrients just as it did in the compost heap. The speed with which this inoculation occurs is rapid and within several months from its first application it can penetrate down into the soil sufficiently far so that plants will reap the benefits of the microbial activity and the nutrients produced. With each application of compost over the seasons the life will spread and reach further and further down into the soil.

Plants deserve a lot more credit than we give them; they produce exudates from their roots which attract the right kind of bacteria, fungi and microbiology to their roots to enable them to get the nutrients they require. Due to the woody or carbon content of your compost, mycorrhizal fungi will be encouraged into the soil. Mycorrhizal fungi have a symbiotic relationship with plants; in return for starches and carbohydrates that are released as exudates from the plant the fungi will feed the roots of the plants with proteins and minerals from up to several metres away. A great percentage of plants form relationships with fungi, somewhere in the region between 80 and 95%. Some fungi wrap themselves around the plant roots (Ectomycorrhiza) while others actually penetrate the root system (Endomycorrhiza). Anything we can do to encourage this relationship should be done, anything to prevent this relationship occurring should be stopped. Digging is a practice that can instantly destroy this harmony in the soil; when compost is applied to the soil there is no longer a need to dig since the structure of the soil is improved to such an extent that over a period of time, even heavy soils will turn to a healthy tilth. It goes without saying that chemicals such as fungicides, pesticides, herbicides and chemical fertilisers will destroy the delicate hyphae (fine tentacle like structure) of fungi which penetrate the soil. These hyphae are mostly invisible to the human eye, it is only when they mass together that they become visible and it is no wonder that generally, gardeners are not aware of their presence and the benefits that they bring to plants. In a cubic meter of soil there could be many, many miles of hyphae present!

To Dig in or Mulch?

Miss Bruce recommended that the compost should be lightly forked into the top 4 to 6 inches (10 to 15cm) of soil at a rate of 2.5lb per square yard (approx. 1 Kg per square metre). I will assume that this was compost without any large unfinished items within it. Personally, I prefer to mulch which provides the same benefits as digging in the compost but just takes a little longer for the effects to kick in. The added advantage with mulching is that it retains more moisture within the soil and suppresses the growth of any weed seeds that may have been present on the soil surface. The disadvantage of mulching is that the rate the mulch is applied per square meter is higher than that for applying sieved compost directly into the soil although some volume of compost is removed during sieving. If you are using the compost as a mulch around plants then there is no need to remove the unfinished material from the compost. Mother nature will take over and tough stems or small twigs will disappear over a period of time.

I am in total agreement with Miss Bruce when she advised that you can never apply too much compost and hungry soil and plants need plenty of food. When mulching, it is debatable how much to apply but somewhere between 1"(2.5cm) and 2"(5cm) thick is usually sufficient. For the main flower borders I aim to make two applications of mulch per year; firstly in late winter when the new growth of perennials is starting to push through the soil and the spring bulbs are getting into their stride, the second application is in mid summer when the late summer flowers need an extra boost to put on a good show. In the vegetable plot the beds get a mid winter mulch ready for sowing crops in early spring. Crops that spend a long time in the soil such as parsnips get a later mulching along the row. Transplanted crops such as broccoli and cabbage get a mulching when they are planted out. If compost is in short supply it should be applied in small quantities to each individual plant by working it into the soil immediately surrounding the plant.

No matter what method you use to incorporate the compost to your soil, the end result will be the same. The plants which you grow will have vitality and disease resistance, flower colours will be more vivid and the flowering period will be longer. If you are growing vegetables then you will benefit from better tasting vegetables that will be full of vitality and nutrition. The compost will condition the soil, by the action of earthworms, tiger worms, millipedes, insects, birds and small animals slowly working the humus into the soil and integrating the humus particles with that of the existing media.

Soil Structure Improvement

When we apply well made compost, we are applying humus. Humus is the debris that consists of countless millions of dead bacteria, protozoa, nematodes, worms, decomposed plant material and complex carbon chains. These chains have a large surface area and hold a negative electrical charge which attract and hold onto positively charged minerals in the soil. No matter what your soil type is, the compost will combine with it to provide it with what it lacks. If you have a clay type soil then the compost will eventually, mainly due to the action of worms, be worked into the lumps of clay, breaking up the adhesion between the fine clay particles thus opening up the structure of the soil. The action of bacteria, fungi and worms produce sticky carbohydrate substances called polysaccharides that act like glue in binding mineral particles with humus. This forms small clumps of material called aggregates and these open up the soil preventing the mineral molecules binding together as they do in clay. The formation of aggregates also creates a more porous structure which allows better drainage but also creates a large surface area for water and soluble nutrients to cling to by capillary action. It is this capillary action in soils which is vital in supplying moisture and nutrients to plants. It is also extremely beneficial in boosting the water retentive capacity of the soil and reduces the amount of watering by rainfall or otherwise that plants require. In very dry spells clay soils can go extremely hard and crack open, this will not happen with compost fed clay soil.

In the same manner, in a silty or sandy soil, the aggregates created will retain more moisture and improve its water retentive capacity. Adding humus to these types of soils prevents erosion because the small mineral particles are glued to humus and are kept moist by the capillary water.

As creatures such as worms, nematodes, beetles and slugs move through the soil looking for food, they create tunnels and spaces between the aggregates and mineral particles. Fungi also infiltrate the soil and the formation of all these spaces between the aggregates allows root growth to penetrate and search out food and moisture.

Sieving

If the compost is to be used in a potting mixture or worked into the soil then it is best to remove any unfinished material by sieving since the breakdown of unfinished compost when mixed in with the soil can rob the soil of nitrogen (bacteria need both carbon and nitrogen to do their work and will tie up the nutrients in their bodies until they die or are eaten and the nutrients released as waste products). Sieving can be carried out using several different types of sieve. For small amounts such as a bucketful, a small plastic 20cm diameter sieve with a 1cm mesh can be used. These are cheap and easily available.

Even more cheaply, and probably free, I have seen people use the rectangular plastic stackable boxes that vegetables are stored in, which have a mesh size of approximately 1cm.

For larger amounts such as a sackful, it is worth investing in a rotasieve which has a rotating arm to assist in the sieving process. They are approximately 40cm in diameter and have a mesh size of 2.5cm x 1cm.

The ultimate sieving device for the composter is the motorised rotating sieve which is quite expensive (approximately £400) but are a worthwhile investment if you make lots of compost. The one I have has 2 mesh sizes; 1cm and 2cm. If the material is quite moist then the 2cm sieve is best since this will not get clogged

Sieving the compost using a plastic storage box for vegetables.

Sieving the compost using a motorised rotating sieve.

up so easy. The inclined drum rotates at a slow speed and material is put into the top end of the sieve using a shovel. The rejected material drops out the bottom end and the compost falls through the mesh into a wheel barrow or container placed underneath. They work really well and a lot of compost can be sieved in a short space of time.

The rejected, unfinished material which is obtained from the compost as a result of sieving can be added to the next compost heap.

Using the Compost as a Potting Mixture

For general potting compost, sieved compost can be mixed 2 parts compost, to 5 parts loam. For seed compost the mixture should be 2 part sieved compost, 5 part loam, 1 part sand and 1 part vermiculite. These are the recipes as recommended by Miss Bruce and have produced good results

Growing Tomato Plants in Pots

The following method is recommended by Miss Bruce and has been included for completeness; however, I have never attempted to implement it myself as yet. For pot grown tomato plants, plant the tomato in the pot using the potting mixture so that the plant pot is approximately half full.

When the roots appear on the surface of the compost, apply 2" (5cm) of top dressing and subsequent dressings each time the roots appear on the surface as follows:

1st dressing:	4 parts loam to 3 parts compost
2nd dressing:	3 parts loam to 4 parts compost
3rd dressing:	2 parts loam to 5 parts compost

When the first truss has set and the tomatoes are golf ball size, use pure compost. When the fruit is ripening, apply either manure or compost water every ten days. When the roots grow out of the drainage holes, put compost on the shelving or staging where the pots are stood.

Making a Manure Tub

If you can get your hands on some fresh cow manure, then you can make a very useful plant food and additive to make your compost more fertile and break down more easily. Obtain some fresh cow pats, then sink a container such as a wooden barrel into the ground so that ground level is about 15cm (6in) from the top of the barrel. It is preferable to use wooden containers but if these are not available then a plastic container with drainage holes should suffice (I used an old plastic dustbin). Fill the container with the cow pats until it is level with the ground and apply approximately 90ml (3 fl.oz.) of Q.R. activator to the manure and cover with a wooden board (I put the dustbin lid on). The manure will be ready to use in about 3 weeks but will look as though there has been no change, it will maintain its fresh appearance, and it will lose the smell of fresh cow manure. The manure will remain in this state for many years according to Miss Bruce. A trowelful of the manure added to a bucket of rainwater (5litre) will make a stock solution. A pint from the stock solution added to a bucket of water will make a dosage solution. This can be applied directly to the soil around plants as a food rich in nutrients. The solution can also be applied to give new life to old apple trees. Holes are made in the ground using a fork (like tinning holes in a lawn) in a circle around the tree, the radius of the circle being equal to the distance that the branches extend from the tree. The manure solution is then poured down the holes. The solution can be added to semi ripe compost heaps to increase their fertility by watering the solution over the heap with a watering can fitted with a rose. If straw is added to the heap it can be pre-soaked in the solution to ensure that the straw fully breaks down during the composting process.

If you can obtain some old dried cow pats, then carry out the procedure as for the fresh manure tub. The process will take about 6 weeks and will produce very dark sweet smelling compost. This is very fertile and can be applied as a top dressing around plants.

The Results of Using the Compost

In the relatively brief time of several years that I have been making Q.R. compost, and as I have already explained in the Introduction and Chapter 2, the results have been miraculous with the garden taking on a whole new feel, the structure of the soil has been completely transformed and success has prevailed in the flower, fruit and vegetable gardens where previously most of my gardening efforts ended up in failure. Although my gardening habits have been organic for over ten years, the last 3 to 4 years where I have been successfully making Q.R compost have been the years where my organic gardening has become increasingly successful. This is no strange coincidence. Without the fundamental tool of the compost heap (or manure) the organic garden is a very tough customer to satisfy. The ancient 'rule of return' is an elementary law of nature that we cannot afford to ignore.

In my case the Q.R. compost system has brought about dynamic changes in the appearance and vitality of the garden in the areas where the compost has been used. The improvement in the gardens fertility and increased diversity of life are noted more and more each year and yet it seems strange to say that I feel that its fertility is still in its infancy and the best is yet to come. My borders are now regularly ravaged by birds and animals seeking out the bountiful supplies of insects and worms that they yield. On the rare occasions that I dig, every spadeful of soil unearths a healthy selection of soil life; millipedes, centipedes, beetles, spiders, woodlice and other creatures are seen with increasing regularity. A robin often follows me around the garden because it knows that where I dig or plant it will be rewarded with a lush meal. Small pleasures such as these make it all worthwhile. For the last 2 years I have hardly touched the hosepipe to water the garden and yet nothing has suffered except a young holly tree which was not given any compost. The major difference that is made to the garden is completely subtle in the way it evolves. Slowly the realisation takes place that the garden requires less work, needs less weeding, needs less watering, needs no (organic or otherwise) fertilisers such as manure, needs no pest controls and needs no bought in growing media. Bonfires of garden waste or disposal of such are not even thought about. In short the garden demands less of the gardener and the outside world and with each of these improvements made to the garden we become one step closer to the fulfilment of a *sustainable organic garden.*

During the course of my research for this book, a telephone call which was made for purposes relating to Miss Bruce's final place of rest bizarrely lead to a discussion about Q.R. compost making. By strange coincidence the lady I spoke to knew about making Q.R. compost, had seen a demonstration and had successfully tried it on her allotment. The demonstration had been given by Julia and William Scott of 'The Walled Garden'; a herb garden in the city of Worcester whish is run entirely on organic principles using Q.R. compost. Julia informed me how she became a convert to Miss Bruce's method;

"In a second hand bookshop I stumbled across 'From Vegetable Waste to Fertile Soil" by Maye Bruce, just at the time when (in the 1970's) when I was deciding to change to organic growing techniques for my herb garden and vegetable patch.

The decision to throw away the chemicals was making me quite nervous, particularly as, at the time, I struggled to make good compost. I was very aware that I was going to need to feed the soil constantly if the changes in my gardening techniques were going to be successful.

Having read her book I collected, grew and dried the herbs. After a year of re-reading the book I made up my first compost heap using the herbs as Maye Bruce described. I was somewhat amazed at the ease of the process and the excellent resulting compost. Even more important, as I fed the soil with the compost I could see the improvement of the soil texture and the growth of the plants.

Over the years, here in the Walled Garden, I have expanded my compost heaps as I got into the rhythm and luxury of having a continuous supply of perfect compost to feed the herb, flower and vegetable gardens. Now, all these years later, I am very aware that I could not have gardened so successfully if it were not for Maye Bruce's inspiring work and publications."

'The Walled Garden' has appeared on many TV and radio programmes, including *Gardener's World, The Flying Gardener and Rick Steins Fresh Food.* Articles about the garden and its plants have appeared in many Journals including, *The Garden* and *The Kitchen Garden.* It is open each summer for the National Garden Scheme; see the 'Yellow Book' for current opening times.

Lady Iliffe from Berkshire is passionate about her composting and commends the method as follows;

"I first used Q.R. in the early 1970's. It was after a visit to Le Vasterival near Dieppe (in France), the garden created by the Princess Sturdza. She was extremely enthusiastic about the importance of compost and when she said it was possible to make it in six weeks I returned home determined to try. I bought a leaflet by Maye E. Bruce called "Compost Making – The Quick Return Method" and followed the instructions and sure enough it is possible to make sweet smelling well balanced compost quickly. This little booklet, last published in 1953, should never be out of print and I cannot think why it is when 'organic' is currently all the rage. I have read quite a lot about compost and in my view this leaflet is far and away the best to follow. It is short, concise, easy to read, interesting and it works.

There is nothing more satisfying than collecting all your suitable material and spending a couple of hours putting it through the shredder and filling your bin. It is hard work but when the job is done I know I have put all my waste material to good use – rather like a cook feels when she has created a delicious meal out of leftover scraps in the kitchen."

Whilst my search for reports from modern day Q.R. composters has resulted in less than a handful, I am sure there are many thousands of people out there, judging from the sales of the thousands of packets of Q.R. powder that Chase sell each year, whom can vouch for its integrity and performance. I hope I have the opportunity to meet and hear from more people in the future with regard to their Q.R. composting experiences (hopefully good ones but I am also interested to hear of any less than successful reports too).

Of the multitude of letters, reports, articles, reviews and references to the performance and usage of the Q.R composting system, many of which are detailed in Miss Bruce's books, I wish to quote a couple of these from independent sources which may be of interest:

L. F. Easterbrook, the agricultural correspondent of the newspaper 'The News Chronicle' had this to say about Miss Bruce's Q.R. method: 'Meanwhile I had heard about Miss Bruce from a relative of hers. I went off and saw her in Gloucestershire. I saw the miserable little film of soil overlaying the relentless Cotswold rock that must make her garden one of the most unpromising sites for horticulture that could be found in England. But, I also saw the magnificent crops growing on it. There were great cabbages of what I can only call a rich "vitamin green" in colour, asparagus stems that looked like young saplings, and flowers of such lovely rich colours that people came from miles around to look at them. Later indoors, I discovered that the taste of those vegetables was every bit as good as their looks, and their size was allied with some of the most tender and succulent vegetables I have ever enjoyed". The article was included in the 1949 publication 'Organic Husbandry, A Symposium'.

Jocelyn Chase of Chase Organics recommended the use of Q.R. activator in his book 'Cloche Gardening' as follows; "The best (compost activator) in my opinion being a herbal preparation known as Q.R. (Quick Return). ...There seems to be no doubt that this activator enormously encourages bacterial action and hastens the decomposition of the heap which breaks down evenly so that there is no necessity to turn it."

CHAPTER 9

The History and Role of Chase Organics in Q.R. Compost Making

The following chapter is set out to explain a brief history of Chase Organics, which has previously been unrecorded, and to establish the knowledge of their involvement in making Q.R. composting successful. Chase Organics have played a vital role in the history of Q.R. compost making through the manufacture and supply of Q.R. compost activator for over 60 years, continuing to the present day. Compost, made using the Q.R. method, and cloches, which were made by Chase, were perfect partners and this relationship featured heavily in the company's beliefs and practices. Chase have also played a pioneering role of major significance as ambassadors of the organic brand; as a company and also through the participation of Jocelyn Chase in the organic movement from the 1940's with his involvement in the Soil Association. As suppliers of organic gardening products, they have contributed to the increase in organic gardening and in maintaining availability of organic seeds, seaweed products, compost and gardening supplies to the organic gardener. It is for the preceding reasons, as well as being extremely interesting and part of our organic gardening heritage, that I have given such attention to the history and business of the company within this book. With their kind cooperation, the following information was mainly provided by Ron Silver, managing director of Chase between 1962 and 1983 and Mike Hedges, the current Managing Director during interviews in the autumn of 2007.

'Chase Protected Cultivation' was first established in Liverpool in 1912 by Major L.H. Chase, an Australian engineer and entrepreneur. He had designed and built many railway bridges in Australia where he was apparently almost treated like royalty, being awarded a 'golden pass' to travel on the railways which were usually only issued to Kings, Queens and Prime Ministers! He moved to England where he planned and constructed the Mersey Transporter Bridge in 1905 over the river Mersey between Widnes and Runcorn (near Liverpool). Major Chase had originally designed the glass and wire

Chase Cloche to protect his lettuces from the industrial grime of the city, and soon realised that it improved growth as well. This innovation soon grew into a commercial success.

In the 1920's he moved to the London area when, with his cloche business established, he became involved with Barnes-Wallis and the ill fated R101 airship project. Major Chase apparently expressed concerns about the design and left the project due to them. Sadly, he was later proved to be exactly right when the airship crashed in 1930, killing 48 people.

Around this time the Chase business moved to Pond House in Chertsey, historically a town whose economy was based on agriculture and market gardening; the perfect location to develop his Cloche business. In those days the company was known as 'Chase Protected Cultivation' and Cloches were the flagship product of the company. The business expanded rapidly and became a significant presence in the area.

Several different types of Cloche were made by Chase including a tomato cloche which was 24" (60cm) high and were used to grow tomatoes and grape vines under them. They also marketed a 'Woolworths Cloche', specifically made for and sold by Woolworths, which was a basic sort of tent type cloche with a single ridge. However the main stalwart of the range was the Chase Large Barn Cloche, and rows of these became a familiar sight throughout the UK.

The Grange Gardens at Chertsey, an area of about 8 acres, were purchased in 1942 as trial experimental grounds which consisted of horticultural land, orchard, kitchen gardens, tennis court and grass paddocks. The main office outgrew the premises at Pond House and was moved to the Grange. Chase owned many properties in the centre of Chertsey particularly in Guildford Street, where they located their accounts office, Cowley House. Additional development included the acquisition of the stretch of land between Guildford Street and St Ann's field, including Gogmore farm, a total area approaching 2 square kilometres and their 'empire' was further increased by the ownership of 45 acres at Lyne. Most of the land acquired by Chase was put to horticultural use and in its hay-day, the Chase establishment at Chertsey was a centre of excellence for organic horticulture with trial fields, seed cultivation and market garden.

Major Chase died during the Second World War and the business was then handed

A 'Dig for Victory' poster issued by the New Zealand government during WW2. The slogan was allegedly coined by Loftus Tottenham one of the co-directors of Chase Organics.
(Image courtesy of the Imperial War Museum)

over to his son, Jocelyn, (J.L.H. Chase) who was one of the founder members of the Soil Association and wrote two books 'Cloche Gardening' and 'Commercial Cloche Gardening'. Like his father, Jocelyn had served in the army but had retired after injury. He had a remarkable ability to quickly learn languages and was fluent in several including French, German, Arabic and Spanish.

During the Second World War, Chase originated many slogans such as 'Cloches v Hitler' with others evolving during their many advertising campaigns. Shortly after the outbreak of the war, the government launched the 'Grow More Food' campaign but this was a complete flop and the government quickly adopted the famous 'Dig for Victory' slogan which, as we know, was a raging success story. According to Ron; it was Chase who originally came up with the memorable 'Dig for Victory' slogan which the government then took over. The slogan was allegedly coined by Loftus Tottenham, one of the co-directors of Chase, who may have passed it onto the government through his connections with them; as mentioned earlier, government officials such as the Minister of Supply are known to have visited Chase's Chertsey establishment. I was informed by Ron that the radio programme "In Your Garden" regularly discussed 'continuous' cloches (they weren't allowed to say Chase because that would be advertising) and also launched the 'Dig for Victory' campaign. There are several different accounts about the origins of the 'Dig for Victory' slogan and it may well be that we never get to discover the full story, but one thing is for sure; it was one of the most successful campaigns of the war, completely surpassing the expectations at the government, and created a transition from dependency to self sufficiency which involved the effort of almost every family in the nation.

Loftus Tottenham appears to have been quite a prominent character with connections in several contemporary walks of life. Ron revealed that he also had a military background and may have carried out undercover assignments in Eastern Europe during WW2. After the war he also had influence in the football world where he ran the 'Chase of Chertsey' football team. There were enough Chase employees to field several teams on a Saturday, and their youth team was also known as 'Arsenal Juniors'. Famous individuals who played for this team in their teens include Ken Bates (ex Chelsea chairman now at Leeds United) and Dave Basset (ex Wimbledon and Sheffield United manager), Ron declared.

After WW2, Chase were approached by the government to provide help for the re-inhabitation of the island of Alderney in the Channel Islands, since the island had been evacuated and turned into a prisoner of war camp during the war. Ron Silver had recently re-joined the company after serving in the Royal Navy and he and a colleague called Passmore were sent out to establish horticultural and agricultural industries on the island in an effort to re-employ the people that wanted to return there and live. It had been decided in England that the island would be run as a communal farm for the first 2 years. However the local people didn't want the government involved and in 1947 a wealthy Birmingham businessman by the name of Francis Impey took over the scheme and Ron started to work under his direction. The project was very successful, implementing the Q.R. method for making compost which was applied to the soil in which the crops were grown. Francis Impey bought an old Fort (Fort Corblets), with a fair amount of land, which he renovated into a comfortable home. Under Francis Impey, Ron started up a cooperative market garden, 'Island Gardens Ltd', because there were too many small growers and individually they would not have been able to market their produce. At first, the market garden was run from the fort and subsequently from Valley Gardens in the Pre de l'Eglise. There were crops of asparagus, melons, strawberries, radishes and flowers, some of which were grown under cloches. The horticultural trade from Alderney continued to thrive until the early sixties, exporting produce and flowers to UK markets. However increasing transport costs, a reduction in boat services and increasing competition from subsidised production in the UK and Europe quashed Alderney's grip on the market.

Jersey had problems circa 1948 when the tomato crop failed. They saw what Ron had achieved on Alderney so they asked him if he could repeat the exercise on Jersey and an experimental station was set up to grow tomatoes. Lots of Q.R. compost was made on Jersey using chaff from the threshing station at the farm where he was working and poultry manure from a large poultry farm. However this gave them some problems because there was too much poultry manure which would produce too much nitrogen in the compost. It was also during this period that Ron learned about the value of using seaweed in horticulture from the Channel Islands growers, and the development of Chase's seaweed products followed on from this.

Chase held "Open Days" for amateurs and growers and these were held every year between 1945 and 1961. The attendance usually varied between 500 and 1000 and special trains were laid on to accommodate the visitors. On one occasion when an Amateurs' Open Day was held on Whit Monday over 4000 people turned up. Special days were organised when Chase would invite Soil Association members and displays were made of their composting methods, soil blocks and foliar sprays. Guest speakers were invited to attend and included Maye E. Bruce, George Copley a Lancastrian garden writer, Dr. E. Pfeiffer from the Biodynamic Association, Lady Eve Balfour the founder of the Soil Association, Lawrence Hills the founder of the Henry Doubleday Research Association (now known as Garden Organic), Dr. Hugh Sinclair a famous nutritionalist and Basil Furneaux who was a soil expert. The Grange Gardens played a large part in spreading interest in organic gardening throughout the world. Trainees and growers would travel from all over the world to learn Chase's organic methods. Chase also invited politicians and were visited by MP's from the House of Commons (in 1946), the Minister of Supply, Conservative and Labour party MP's and councillors.

Chase became quite a large organisation employing hundreds of people in the trial fields, market garden and manufacturing the cloches which were sold all over the world. In the days when people would go on company outings to the seaside, Chase would have their annual trip to Bournemouth and on these occasions the whole town would close down. Ron described it as "A weird sort of place to be on that particular day. I remember Mr Bush who was the owner of the local delicatessen used to get furious because all his customers were gone".

Visitors inspecting the compost at the Grange. *(Courtesy of Chase Organics)*

Produce from the gardens was mostly marketed at Brentford in west London and was always labelled as 'Compost Grown'. Very often a consignment would be sold before it reached the market because of the consistently high quality. During 1961, 'Wholefood' in London's Baker Street was supplied with produce including strawberries, lettuce and runner beans. 'Wholefood' was a shop set up by Mary Langman, one of the founders of the Soil Association, as a means for organic suppliers to sell their organic produce through and was the first establishment of its kind.

Miss Bruce had been looking for a 'soil-conscious corporation' to take over production of the Q.R. compost activator in order to ensure that there was both continuity of supply and to avoid reliance on a single source. By chance and good fortune, Jocelyn visited Miss Bruce after he had seen the effects of the compost on his Worcestershire garden. He became interested in the activator and how it worked, eventually using it in his own garden and exhibiting samples of the compost at one of Chase's shows in Chertsey.

In February 1946, Miss Bruce attended the Cloche Exhibition at the Horticultural

Hall in Vincent Square. This was one of two occasions where Chase took over the whole of the hall to exhibit their products. It was at this exhibition that Jocelyn agreed to take on the manufacture and distribution of the Q.R. compost activator.

Chase's manufacturing partner for Q.R. Compost Activator were manufacturing chemists William Ransom & Son, based in Hitchin, Hertfordshire and the herbs were grown on Ransoms' land. The company had the idea of mechanically grinding the activator powder which made it much finer than Miss Bruce could make with her pestle and mortar, making a further improvement to the performance of the Q.R. compost activator. Ransoms continued to make Q.R. and Chase Seaweed Extracts until their plant in the centre of Hitchin closed in 2004, since when new partners have been found who continue to make the products to Chase's specifications.

Q.R. compost activator was sold by Chase in many countries including Australia, Canada, New Zealand and South Africa. In particular, thousands of packets were shipped to Australia. In Canada it was sold under the name 'ACTO', possibly derived from the word 'activator'.

Jocelyn Chase used to do lectures all over the country; Gogmore farm being regularly used for demonstrations on how to make Q.R. compost. Some films were also made but the whereabouts of these is not known. Apparently Miss Bruce did not attend any lectures with Chase.

Chase had their own composting department and would make up to 2000 tons of compost a year. Everything was composted with little farmyard manure available so the Q.R. method of composting (which didn't require manure) was used with great success. The compost was made in large open heaps on the headlands bordering their fields ready for distribution onto the crops. Although turning was not advocated by Miss Bruce, Ron explained that the open type heaps were turned (using machinery) because the outside wouldn't decompose. Some of the compost heaps were edged with bales of straw which would eventually rot down and be turned into the compost. Composting material came from many places, including sewage sludge from a local sewage farm. Ron also advised "We used to use all the coffee residues from Nescafe, tons of it, that's the stuff you want to use if you want to keep worms. The compost was absolutely thick with worms; you could almost see the compost going out to the fields on its own". Compost was also made from the weed thrown on the banks of the local rivers and the Basingstoke canal when they were cleared out annually and large quantities of spent mushroom manure were obtained from a mushroom farm. All these different materials gave them a very good mixture to work with and compost was made using the Q.R. method which was sold in hardware and seed shops under the name of 'GRO'. The composting department at Chase was run by John Marshall, an ex-army captain. Many ex-military people were employed by Chase after the Second World War ended.

As a firm believer and user of the Q.R. composting method, Jocelyn's opinion was that composting and cloches went hand in hand. In an article he wrote for the winter 1948/1949 edition of *Mother Earth,* the journal of the Soil Association, he explains this relationship, "In cloche gardening, more crops are taken from the ground within the year, and so the need for humus is more vital." He added, "It (compost) darkens the surface soil which therefore absorbs a greater proportion of the sun's rays and so rises in temperature. This means quicker germination and better root development. The chief reason is that a high humus content is necessary to increase the speed of lateral

The minister of Supply visiting the Grange. Loftus Tottenham is on the left, Jocelyn Chase is in the centre. *(Courtesy of Chase Organics)*

water movement in the soil....it is no exaggeration to say that cloche cultivation depends entirely on lateral water movement in the soil for its success. This movement seems to depend almost directly on the humus content." (The implication here was that watering carried out either side of the cloche would provide, by lateral movement of the water through the soil, sufficient water for the plants underneath the cloche and hence removing the requirement to lift the cloches for watering). He also stated, "The hazards of disease, under-nourishment and lack of moisture are greatly reduced by the compost."

Interestingly, an experiment was set up at Chertsey to determine whether digging was beneficial or not. There were two plots; a no-dig plot where there was no digging for several years running and a plot where routine digging was carried out. According to Ron there was little difference in the results obtained between the two plots.

Jocelyn was a great believer in dowsing (the technique of finding water without the use of scientific apparatus) and had a dowsing contact, A. R. Kent at Kemble in Gloucestershire, who would use his techniques to determine whether a product was any good or not before it was put on sale. Jocelyn was also a keen believer in homeopathy which may in some way have assisted in his faith in the use of the Q.R. composting method; akin to homeopathy with the small amounts of activator powder used.

Ron advised that by the 1950's, Q.R. compost powder was sold by virtually every ironmonger and horticultural establishment in England. Chase had as many as ten 'reps' on the road visiting all the hardware and seed shops, some of which sold vast quantities of the Q.R. activator; sales were at their highest in the Southern counties, particularly in Suffolk, though not so good in the north of England. During this period Ron Silver was a Sales Representative and Horticultural Advisor for the south west of England, a job he thoroughly enjoyed, covering a large area between Bournemouth in the east and the tip of Cornwall in the west and going north as far as Dudley in the Midlands.

Chase's seed business had been in existence since the 1940's, growing and processing their own seeds at The Grange in Chertsey and eventually in other areas, including Essex. In particular it is known that some lettuce seed was produced in Alderney.

By the late 1950's, the Cloche business had started to decline as plastics and polythene became cheaper to produce so it was sold off along with some other parts of the business to a company called Expandite.

Jocelyn was an ambassador of organic horticulture but his travelling and promotional works were detrimental to the business. He was a very generous man, but over the years he made some bad appointments and decisions and the company started to suffer, literally to the point of collapse. By 1961, Jocelyn had also sold the seed business and much of the property and land owned by Chase, and eventually emigrated to Argentina. He remained the major shareholder and non executive director. Ron Silver, who was by this time Sales Manager for the whole of Chase was appointed Managing Director of the newly formed Chase Organics (GB) Ltd in 1962 to lead the recovery of the remaining parts of the company.

Chase now decided to concentrate on Q.R. and seaweed products. As referred to earlier, this started when Ron was working in Jersey after WW2. Chase were originally sellers of 'Maxicrop' but later developed, together with William Ransom, their own unique seaweed extract known as Sea Magic. In 1958 this had been renamed SM3 and has been used ever since with great success, becoming the company's main product through to the 1990's, selling to farmers and growers in UK and as far afield as Florida, Chile and Australia. A new head office and warehouse building was purchased in Shepperton, Middlesex during this time. This was a relatively quiet period in the company's history, as the "glamour days" of the time in Chertsey were left behind. According to Ron, many of the buildings that Chase owned have now been demolished and been built on or developed; Pond House was replaced with a large office block which has remained empty for the last five years. The original house was built on the site of a large pond and that's why it was called Pond House. The Grange at Chertsey is now a nursing home.

The seed business continued to be run as "Chase Compost Grown Seeds" by Reid and Manette Baillie who previously owned a seed shop called 'Walls of Bath'. The Baillies moved to Benhall, near Saxmundham in Suffolk. They also continued another Chase product, 'glitterbangs' (metallic foil strips which deter birds, rabbits and deer from approaching crops by a combination of rattling and reflection). In 1983, the Baillies decided to retire and Ron brought the seed business back, employing a young graduate, Mike Hedges.

Mike's first job was to live in for three months with the Baillies and learn about every

The following inscription was written on the back of this photograph:
A section of the Experimental Grounds at Chertsey: in the foreground, cloches; then a belt of open experimental ground where trees, plants and shrubs are going through 'comparative' tests; on the summit of the hill begins a belt of cloche tests which stretch far over the other side, while under the cloches on all sides fruits and vegetable, such as strawberries and lettuces, are grown throughout winter: fresh strawberries at Christmas for instance are annually a 'staff treat'.
(Courtesy of Chase Organics)

Open Day Visitors. *(Courtesy of Chase Organics)*

aspect of the business, before it was moved back to Chase's premises in Shepperton.

Mike remembers the day when Lady Eve Balfour visited Benhall to buy her seeds. She marched in waving her walking stick, informing Mr Baillie in no uncertain terms that he had made an error in the catalogue, describing a plant as an annual when it was in fact a perennial! Mike saw that even as an old lady, Lady Eve had a very commanding presence.

In 1994 Jocelyn Chase returned to live in the UK. He was still the majority shareholder, and had decided he wanted to become involved with running the company again at the age of 84! Sadly this led to Ron's resignation as Managing Director, and Jocelyn took the position for a few months until he realised he was unable to do the job at such an advanced age. The company was sold to Ian Allan Group, a thriving local company, in the Printing, Publishing and Travel management industries. Ian Allan had been a director of Chase for several years and saw the opportunity to develop the SM3, Q.R. and Seed businesses. Ron remained as a consultant for several years. Jocelyn died a couple of years later in Happisburgh, Norfolk where he lived with his sister.

The company continued to thrive and expand under Richard Rixson who was appointed Managing Director. In 1991, Richard set up a partnership with the charity Henry Doubleday Research Association (now Garden Organic), to run a joint mail order seed and organic gardening catalogue. This signalled the start of a major expansion in the seed business that originated all those years ago in Chertsey. Since then there has been a steady increase in the commercial availability of organically grown seeds and the catalogue is now recognised as a leading source of these. In 2004 Richard retired as MD, but continues to work part time for Chase Organics, and was succeeded by Mike Hedges, who has continued in enhancing and developing the business into its current successful position.

Today the core business of Chase is *The Organic Gardening Catalogue,* though Q.R., SM3 and its more concentrated version, SM6, continue to be important products.

During his career Ron says he made many good friends and has been fortunate enough to travel to over fifty countries in his work. He has made Q.R. compost for many years and still continues to do so despite now being in his mid 80's. When I asked him if he had any hints, tips or trade secrets he told me "It always turns out good as long as you get a good mix of material" and he added, "It used to heat up within twelve hours. I

Visitors next to tomato cloches, 11th April 1946. *(Courtesy of Chase Organics)*

A composting demonstration at Gogmore Farm attracts an inquisitve audience.
(Courtesy of Chase Organics)

remember we had a show at Doncaster racecourse and we made a compost heap, we cut the grass around the racecourse and made compost. We had a thermostat made out of an old pole that came out of an aeroplane and pushed it into the centre, people would come and have a look at it and see what the high temperature was. In a matter of hours we got the heat up".

When Ron was asked whether he agreed with Miss Bruce in that vegetables grown in Q.R. compost taste better than others he replied, "I think she was right, I think organically grown vegetables are better, well I'm positive they are. A crop you can really test for it is tomatoes because they respond very quickly to what you're putting on them. I can remember saying that some tomatoes tasted bloody terrible! Others would taste lovely and sweet and that was the difference"

Mike has used the Q.R. composting method for about twenty years now and advised, "When I first started working for Chase I knew very little about gardening, but I was inspired by the Baillies and Ron and soon had two allotments near my home. I have never used anything but Q.R. to make my compost. In the early days I remember the soil was poor and many plants suffered from pests and diseases. These have decreased over the time I have been growing using my own compost to improve the soil and have now all but disappeared. If you improve the structure and fertility of the soil, everything else follows on naturally"

Chase Organics are still the sole supplier and manufacturer of Q.R. compost activator and it can be ordered through the *Organic Gardening Catalogue*:

Online: www.OrganicCatalogue.com
Or by phone: 0845 130 1304.

Bibliography

It is my intention to give acknowledgement to the authors and works I have consulted in the writing of this book and in the instances where this has been omitted from the text for ease of reading, I trust that inclusion of the following sources in this bibliography will be accepted as acknowledgement.

Quick Return Compost Making:

Bruce, Maye E. *From Vegetable Waste to Fertile Soil* Faber & Faber, Second impression 1943

Bruce, Maye E. *Common-Sense Compost Making By the Quick Return Method* Faber & Faber, Sixth impression 1953.

Bruce, Maye E. *Common-Sense Compost Making By the Quick Return Method* Faber & Faber, New Edition by the Soil Association 1967.

The Rule Of Return and the Hunza Tribe:

Philip Conford *The Origins of the Organic Movement* Floris Books, 2001

Theory of How the Compost Heap Works:

Jeff Lowenfels & Wayne Lewis *Teaming with Microbes – A Gardener's Guide to the Soil Food Web* Timber Press, 2006

Clare Foster *Compost* Cassel Illustrated, 2002

Materials and Their Addition to the Heap:

Billington, F.H. *Compost For Garden Plot Or Thousand-Acre Farm* Faber & Faber, Third impression 1943

Herbs and Their Uses:

Nicholas Culpeper *Culpeper's Complete Herbal* W. Foulsham & Co. Ltd.

Gertrud Franck *Companion Planting* Thorsons Publishing Group, 1983

Richard Craze *Herbal Teas* Courage Books, 1998

Claire Lowenfeld *Herb Gardening* Faber & Faber, 1973

Jochen Bockemuhl & Kari Jarvinen *Extraordinary Plant Qualities For Biodynamics* Floris Books, 2005

Richard Mabey *Flora Britanica* Chatto & Windus, 1997

The Role of Chase Organics in Q.R. Compost Making:

Chase, J.L.H. *Cloche Gardening* Faber & Faber, Third impression 1952

Peak Oil:

The Soil Association *One Planet Agriculture - The Case For Action* (Booklet)

General:

Various Authors *Organic Husbandry* Easter 1949

Websites:

History of Chase Organics
www.ianallan.com/group.html
www.islandlife.org/history_ald_bjbonnard2.htm
www.visitalderney.com/flora_fauna/
www.mersey-gateway.org/server.php?show=ConGallery.17

Lord Roberts National Service League
www.Kipling.org.uk/rg_lordroberts_moore.htm

The Bruce Family and Norton Hall (CADHAS website)
www.chippingcampdenhistory.org.uk/notes-queries/sam-bruce

The Countryside Agency
http://Cms.ed.countrysideaccess.gov.uk/layout/set/print/content/view/full/84

The Healing powers of Honey
www.bupa.co.uk/health_information/asp/healthy_living/lifestyle/diet/honey/
www.worldwidewounds.com/2001/november/Molan/honey-as-topical-agent.html

The Hunza Tribe
www.journeytoforever.org/farm_library/medtest/medtest

The Soil Food Web
http://soils.usda.gov/sqi/concepts/soil_biology/soil_food_web.html

The Eastern Sage
www.peterrussell.com/SG/Ch8.php

Q.L.I.F. Food Survey
www.timesonline.co.uk/tol/news/uk/health/article2753546.ece

Oak Tree
www.icons.org.uk/the icons/collection/oak-tree/biography/oak-tree-the-basic
www.treeregister.org/historical.shtml

Index

In 1935, Maye E. Bruce innovated her 'Quick Return' compost system as a method for gardeners and farmers alike to make fertile compost in a matter of weeks without turning and without manure. This method has survived to this day as a saviour to the few thousand or so organic followers who 'are in the know'. Well now *the secret* is unleashed and help is available to those gardeners, allotment holders and farmers who have the desire to turn their interests towards a sustainable organic future and convert their vegetative waste into a vitalising and nourishing food for that most valuable asset; the soil.

In doing so, the rewards will bring health to those plants we grow, well being to those who feed on them and a 'vital' contribution towards saving our planet.

£12.95 RRP

ISBN 978-0-9560087-0-1

9 780956 008701 >